COLORADO'S
JAPANESE AMERICANS

COLORADO'S
JAPANESE AMERICANS

From 1886 to the Present

BILL HOSOKAWA

University Press of Colorado

Published by the University Press of Colorado
5589 Arapahoe Avenue, Suite 206C
Boulder, Colorado 80303

 The University Press of Colorado is a proud member of
the Association of American University Presses.

The University Press of Colorado is a cooperative publishing enterprise supported,
in part, by Adams State College, Colorado State University, Fort Lewis College,
Mesa State College, Metropolitan State College of Denver, University of Colorado,
University of Northern Colorado, and Western State College of Colorado.

Library of Congress Cataloging-in-Publication Data

Hosokawa, Bill.
  Colorado's Japanese Americans : from 1886 to the present / Bill Hosokawa.
     p. cm.
  Includes bibliographical references and index.
  ISBN 0-87081-810-4 (hardcover : alk. paper) — ISBN 0-87081-811-2 (pbk. :
alk. paper)
  1. Japanese Americans—Colorado—History. 2. Japanese Americans—Colorado—
Social conditions. 3. Colorado—Ethnic relations. I. Title.
  F785.J3H67 2005
  978.8'004956—dc22

2005011167

Design by Daniel Pratt

Chapter motif photograph: Shingo Nakamura, age twenty-nine, 1917.

CEH Co-winner of the 2005 Colorado Endowment for the Humanities Publication Prize
The CEH Publication Prize annually supports publication of outstanding nonfiction
works that have strong humanities content and that make an area of humanities research
more available to the Colorado public. The CEH Publication Prize funds are shared by the
University Press of Colorado and the authors of the works being recognized. The Colorado
Endowment for the Humanities is a statewide, nonprofit organization dedicated to improving
the quality of humanities education for all Coloradans.

To the Issei, Colorado pioneers from a distant shore

CONTENTS

FOREWORD

Stephen J. Leonard and Thomas J. Noel

As the initial offering in the University Press of Colorado's Timberline Series, we selected Bill Hosokawa's *Colorado's Japanese Americans: From 1886 to the Present*. His work meets our aspirations that the Timberline Series encompass the best works on Colorado.

William Kumpei Hosokawa has made history as well as written it. Bill was born in Seattle in 1915. His father, Setsugo, came from Hiroshima in 1899 at age sixteen to work as a railroad section hand in Montana. By 1913 Setsugo had saved enough money to return to Japan to marry Kimiyo Omura, a schoolteacher. She helped instill in their son, Bill, a love of writing that led him to the University of Washington School of Journalism. There his advisor told Bill that he, as a Japanese, would never get a job at a U.S. newspaper.

Upon graduation, young Hosokawa found work as a secretary at the Japanese consulate in Seattle. This position gave him an opportunity to go with his new wife, Alice Miyake, to Singapore to help establish an English language newspaper, *The Singapore Herald*. After a year in Singapore and travels in Japan, Korea, and China, it seemed obvious to Bill that war was coming. He returned to Seattle, arriving just six weeks before the Japanese bombed Pearl Harbor.

Bill, his wife, and their infant son, along with others were arrested in Seattle simply for being ethnic Japanese and eventually shipped to the relocation camp at Heart Mountain in bleak, windswept northern Wyoming. After fourteen months of persistent effort, Hosokawa finally was granted permission to accept a $35 a week job on the *Des Moines Register* in Iowa. In 1946 Hosokawa applied to *The Denver Post,* which had been relentless in its negative reporting on Japanese Americans before and during World War II. After the war, a new editor, Palmer Hoyt, strove to make the newspaper more positive and progressive. Despite criticism, Hoyt hired Hosokawa. Bill spent thirty-eight years at *The Denver Post,* rising through the ranks from copy editor to makeup editor, wire services editor, executive news editor, assistant managing editor, Sunday editor, editor of *Empire Sunday Magazine,* associate editor, and editor of the editorial page. After his retirement from the *Post* in 1984, the *Rocky Mountain News* hired Bill as their reader's representative. He also taught editorial and magazine writing at University of Colorado, University of Northern Colorado, and University of Wyoming.

Hosokawa wrote the definitive history of *The Denver Post—Thunder in the Rockies* (Morrow, 1976)—and *Nisei* (Morrow, 1969; University Press of Colorado, 2002), the story of second generation Japanese Americans, plus seven other books. A former president of the American Association of Sunday and Feature Editors and founding president of the Colorado Freedom of Information Council, he is enshrined in the Denver Press Club Hall of Fame as well as the

National Cowboy Museum Hall of Fame for the western history he published as editor of *Empire Magazine*. In addition to freelancing for national magazines such as the *Saturday Evening Post* and *Readers' Digest*, he wrote a weekly "Out of the Frying Pan" column for thirty-five years for the Japanese American Citizens League newspaper, the *Pacific Citizen*. He continues to write a weekly column for the *Rocky Mountain Jiho* in Denver, and the *Rafu Shimpo* in Los Angeles.

The Japanese government in 1987 awarded Hosokawa the Order of the Rising Sun for promoting U.S.-Japanese understanding and trade. This quiet, unassuming man has made a tremendous difference with his lucid writing and heroic efforts to right wrongs. Besides capturing the bittersweet Japanese American experience, he has pointed out the importance of clinging to the U.S. Constitution in troubled times.

While at the *Post* but especially after his retirement, Hosokawa has striven tirelessly to promote Japanese American friendship and cultural and trade relations. Morgan Smith, longtime director of the Colorado Department of Local Affairs and a leading proponent of international trade, came to know Hosokawa well. Bill Hosokawa, Smith reports, "prompted the first Colorado trade delegation to Japan which led to the opening of a Colorado office in Tokyo. Bill also spearheaded the establishment of the Japan American Society of Colorado in 1989. Bill, who served as Colorado's honorary Japanese consul, quietly made the case with the Japanese Foreign Ministry for the 1998 establishment of consular offices in Colorado."

Realizing that strong trade and cultural ties would secure friendly relations, Hosokawa helped make Japan the leading oversees market for Colorado as well as a major source of foreign investment in Colorado. Rarely has one man done so much to replace wartime hatred and imprisonment with amicable cultural and trade relations. Furthermore, as this book will show you, Bill has been the foremost reporter and historian of the Japanese Americans in Colorado.

INTRODUCTION

This book is about a people from a rocky string of islands who journeyed eastward across the vast Pacific Ocean and came to Colorado in search of a future for themselves and their children. It is the one-hundred-year history—a significant, warm, and sometimes sad story of hardships, defeats, and successes, of laughter, tears, and ultimate triumphs—of Colorado's Japanese Americans.

The book can trace its origins to one October day in 2003 when my friend Kimiko Side came to see me in her role as president of a public service organization, the Japanese Association of Colorado. She told me the association would be observing the one hundredth anniversary of its founding and a committee had come up with the idea of publishing a book about its history.

And, she said, the association wanted me to write the book.

Why me? I have lived in Colorado for more than fifty years but never paid much attention to the Japanese Association. Too many other things to do.

But, she argued, you are a writer.

Well, yes, sort of.

And, she went on, we are not thinking of a book about the association itself. We're thinking about the people, the Coloradans from Japan and their descendants, the story of their experiences. In other words, a human story.

That was more interesting. Go on, I said.

Among your books, Kimiko continued, was *Nisei*, which did a beautiful job of telling about the Japanese American people in the whole country. Why not a book specifically about Japanese Americans in Colorado—who they were and what they did and why they did the things they did and the problems they faced as Coloradans and how they overcame them?

Interesting idea.

Nisei was the first of about a dozen books I have written, some of which were on the Japanese American experience. *Nisei* had focused on the people in the West Coast states, where perhaps 90 percent of Japanese Americans were living in 1941. It told of their travails during World War II when they were hustled into U.S.-style concentration camps as a result of the federal government's hysterical and tragic assumption that race equated mass disloyalty. Kimiko pointed out that there wasn't much in *Nisei,* or any other book, about the experience of Japanese Americans in the interior of the country and suggested it was time their story be told.

What was their story?

The vast majority of Japanese immigrants eventually had settled in California and Washington with a smaller number in Oregon. But on their arrival, with no knowledge of the English language or American ways, the first jobs for approximately one-third of them were working as unskilled laborers in the inland West maintaining the railroads that stretched to the endless horizon. Not many remained in these jobs for long. The deserts of Arizona, New Mexico, and Utah were too hot; winters in Colorado, Wyoming, and Montana, too fiercely cold for youths from the temperate Japanese homeland. Seeing only a bleak and unpromising future in these states, most headed back to sink their roots near the coast. Only the hardiest few remained inland. Eventually they started farms, which required little in capital but much hard work and love of the soil, and began families.

In 1940, just before tension between Japan and the United States flared into war in the Pacific, the federal census showed 126,947 "Japanese" in the United States, not including Hawaii, which had yet to achieve statehood. Of those, 79,642 were American-born, American-educated Nisei who were U.S. citizens by birth. And 47,305 were Issei of the immigrant generation who remained aliens because the law denied the privilege of naturalization to Asians. Their numbers were never replenished because of the 1924 ban on further immigration from Asia. California was home of the largest number by far of ethnic Japanese. Colorado's Japanese population had not grown significantly since the 1910 census when 2,300 were shown to be in the state with fewer than 600 in Denver. After 1910 the total was relatively stable as Nisei replaced the dwindling number of Issei.

Although the American-born became the majority, they as a group were young and inexperienced in 1940. On the West Coast as well as in Colorado the communities continued to be dominated by the elders. Thus perhaps it was inevitable that, yielding to the fears of the military and the latent anti-Asian hostility of much of the West Coast's establishment, President Franklin D. Roosevelt should sign Executive Order 9066 on February 19, 1942, six weeks after the outbreak of war. It authorized the military in the name of national security to establish zones from which "any or all persons of Japanese ancestry, alien and non-alien" could be excluded, "non-alien" being a cruel euphemism for "citizen." At the time and to the dismay of Japanese Americans, there was virtually no public protest against the arbitrary suspension of the rights of certain Americans based on their ethnicity.

The prohibited zones included the southern half of Arizona, all of California, the western halves of Oregon and Washington, and all of Alaska. And because there was no place for the evacuees to go, concentration camps to house them (euphemistically called "relocation centers") were built hurriedly in the sparsely populated interior. One of the camps was in Colorado and its story is part of this book. The amazing part of this bit of history is the general American public's acceptance—approval might be more accurate—of the arbitrary suspension of rights of certain citizens.

Among Japanese Americans, the great majority accepted the government's actions as their patriotic duty. A small minority protested what they called the majority's willingness to be led like sheep to slaughter, and one aspect of their protest is told in Chapter 13.

The events of the time had a profound effect on Colorado's indigenous Japanese American population. After the war, many of the evacuees, seeing nothing but hostility on the West Coast, chose to remain in Colorado. I was one of the postwar pilgrims. The Japanese American community's social life and economy changed vastly as their numbers quadrupled, the median age dropped, and English became the primary language.

Kimiko Side finally persuaded me to take on the assignment of chronicling this story, with encouragement from many members of the community and the good folks at the University Press of Colorado. I have completed this book with a combination of pleasure, pride, and despair. Pleasure and pride because I think it is an interesting story that deserves recording. And despair because I had neither the time nor the energy to dig as deeply as I needed to uncover the story's every detail.

In accepting the assignment to write the book I specified it would be nothing like the self-laudatory "directories" of two generations ago in which Japanese immigrants paid to be listed. Families bought space in these commercially sponsored publications to boast of their successes so they could assure folks back in Japan that they were doing well. "If you want to see your name in print," I told the Japanese Association sponsors, "you may have to look in the telephone directory. There is so much to our story that I must be extremely selective about what I use; the writer must be given full responsibility for the content." The sponsors were understanding and saw no problem.

I must express gratitude to the many individuals who patiently sat for interviews and dug deep for the documentary material and photographs I sought. They are too numerous to mention by name, but it would be ungrateful not to thank Sam Mayeda, Jim Hada, and George Masunaga, who escorted me on an expedition into the Arkansas Valley in search of information. And I must thank old friend Tom Noel, Colorado's leading historian, who encouraged me to take on the project.

No doubt many serious historians will decry the absence of footnotes in this book. Footnotes are, of course, vital in attributing information in a scholarly history, but they have always bothered me as a reader because they break up the flow of the story. Rather than using footnotes in this historical narrative I have made attribution in the text, newspaper-style, where attribution seemed necessary. Tangential information appears in notes at the end of the book.

I have been given full freedom in writing the book and have tried to exercise it judicially. To those I may have offended or overlooked, *sumimasen, gomennasai, shitsu rei itashimashita,* which are the various ways of apologizing in Japanese. I thank the Japanese Association of Colorado for the opportunity and honor of telling the Colorado story of our people. Members of the association's history project committee are, in alphabetical order, Eiichi Imada, Jim Kanemoto, Mrs. Kimiko Side, Dr. James Terada, and Albert Yamamoto.

Enjoy.

BILL HOSOKAWA
DENVER, 2005

COLORADO'S
JAPANESE AMERICANS

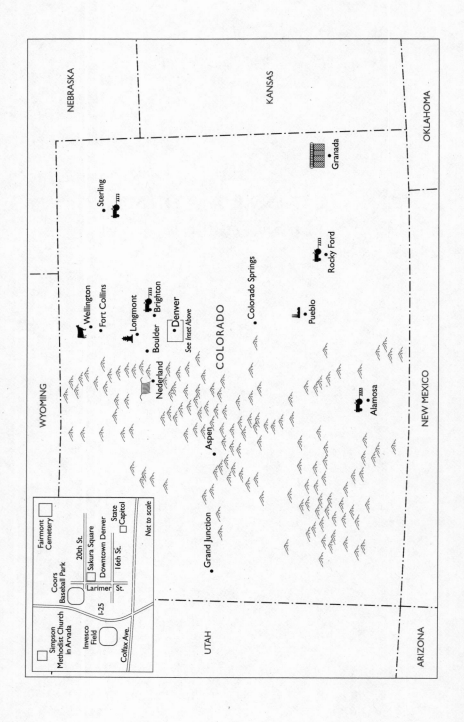

NEBRASKA

KANSAS

OKLAHOMA

WYOMING

Granada

Sterling

Rocky Ford

Wellington
Fort Collins

Longmont
Brighton
Boulder
Denver
See Inset Above

Colorado Springs

COLORADO

Pueblo

Nederland

Aspen

Alamosa

Grand Junction

NEW MEXICO

UTAH

ARIZONA

Simpson
Methodist Church
in Arvada

Fairmont
Cemetery

Coors
Baseball Park

20th St.
Sakura Square
Downtown Denver
16th St.

Larimer St.

State
Capitol

Invesco
Field

I-25

Colfax Ave.

Not to scale

chapter one

THE FIRST
CENTURY

"What," the visitor from Japan asked, "have the Japanese—people from my country and their descendants—what have they done in the century they have been in Colorado to make it a better state, a better place? What have they done for themselves, and for America? What triumphs and difficulties have they had?"

Good questions.

A quick, one-word answer to all of them is "much" despite the fact that the 2000 federal census counted only 11,571 persons of Japanese ancestry living in Colorado, a state of more than 4.3 million. This book attempts to tell the story of the Japanese Americans in Colorado.

In 1886, when Colorado was just emerging from its raw frontier beginnings, a Japanese aristocrat named Matsudaira Tadaatsu appeared on the scene. Matsudaira did not remain long, but he was followed by hundreds of other Japanese, mostly sons of impoverished peasant families from the provinces. They came to be known as the Issei, meaning "first generation." Most had little education but were ambitious. Hardworking and accustomed to privation, they had come to the United States with few intending to remain. Most arrived hoping to make a bit of money before returning to the homeland to buy a few acres of farmland, start a family, and live happily ever after. That ended in 1924 when the United States, in a calculated racial insult, passed legislation prohibiting further immigration from Asia.

This 1924 law, called the Asian Exclusion Act, had a second and unforeseen effect. Besides prohibiting further immigration from Japan, it raised a psychological barrier between the Japanese immigrants and their new homeland. Suddenly they felt cut off from their families back home but unwelcome in their newly adopted country. Some, fearing isolation and increasing hostility in the United States, hurried home. But most of the Issei stayed because, for the first time, they realized how deeply they were rooted in the not always hospitable soil of the new world. Many had acquired the confidence and means to marry, lease or purchase land (where it was not prohibited), and establish homes. Perhaps most significant was the appearance of a generation of U.S.-born and -educated sons and daughters who would be cultural and legal aliens in their ancestral homeland. These were the Nisei, the "second generation." In Colorado, despite drought, depression, and lingering racism, the Issei persevered and watched their children grow.

Seventeen years later the thunder of bombs fell on Pearl Harbor. That earthshaking event led to the forced removal of all Japanese Americans from coastal areas of the West—some 115,000, two-thirds of whom were native-born citizens of the United States—in a panicky defense measure fed by racial prejudice. Some of these exiles found refuge—voluntarily or not—in Colorado, which was otherwise unaffected by the exclusion order.

During winter 1940–1941 Issei residents of the state watched with growing dread as relations between the United States and Japan worsened. Although they lived a thousand miles and several towering mountain ranges from the Pacific coast, what would happen to them if war broke out? Early in 1941 the leaders of the Japanese Association of Colorado—a loosely knit organization that was part benevolent society, part social association, and part struggling watchdog over Issei rights—called a special meeting in Denver for Issei compatriots in Colorado, Wyoming, and Nebraska. The purpose was to discuss their mutual plight. On March 8 and 9, 1941, approximately one hundred Japanese from twenty-four districts assembled in Denver at the offices of the Japanese Association at 2109 Arapahoe Street—a building long gone—for what was described as "a meeting of Japanese in the tri-states area to plan for crisis management."

It was a wide-ranging and often convoluted discussion of perceived problems. No minutes of the meeting have been found. In 1995, however, *Colorado Jijo* magazine published an article about that meeting based largely on the recollections of Rev. Hiram Hisanori Kano who had been there. Father Kano, as he was known, was unusual for an immigrant from Japan. The second son of a nobleman, he was baptized by a Dutch Reformed Church missionary in Japan in 1910. Six years later he traveled to the University of Nebraska to study agricultural economics. Instead of going home with his degree, he moved to western Nebraska where he farmed to support himself while serving as pastor for Japanese in the area. The *Jijo* article said:

> He recalled that the 1941 Denver conference brought out
> discussion on a large number of issues including the education of
> Nisei, the role of Japanese language schools, how to treat the

Japanese flag in the U.S., the proper way to honor Nisei being called into military service by the new draft law,* and the importance of having enough cash on hand to meet emergency needs in case banks froze the accounts of Japanese depositors.

But the most intense discussion had to do with the possibility of mob violence against Japanese in Denver if tensions in Asia continued to escalate. Some remembered stories of a drunken American mob attacking Denver's Chinatown in the 1880s, setting homes afire and terrifying Chinese. More recently there had been an incident outside Peking in North China where, after a Japanese military plane had mistakenly bombed a Chinese city, mob violence had resulted in the death of several hundred Japanese residents.

There were some at the conference who contended that rather than die an inglorious death at the hands of rioters, it was more honorable to take one's own life by plunging a knife into his throat like samurai. Dr. Konai Miyamoto, a dentist who had attended the Japanese Military Academy, was among those who insisted that the honor of the Japanese residents be upheld by whatever means necessary. Ultimately it was agreed that American authorities should be called on to defend the Japanese residents if violence should arrive. Residents of rural areas in particular were urged to keep in contact with the authorities. As a result of the conference, the Issei began a quiet lobbying effort to make their concerns known. State and local officials were contacted by various individuals and told of the fears of Japanese residents.

---

*It was customary in Japan for families and friends to fete young men called up for military duty because it was considered a privilege to serve one's country. At the Denver meeting it was agreed that because the Nisei were being summoned for training—and not going into combat—each community could decide locally how it should honor its draftees.

Unrecorded, but certainly prominent in the minds of these Japanese, was concern about the future of their U.S.-born, U.S.-citizen Nisei sons and daughters, most of whom were minors. If, for instance, members of the Issei were arrested or even deported, what would happen to their children? The Issei generation, particularly in the rural areas, had sacrificed to set up Japanese language schools where their children could learn about the old country. The first words these children had spoken were likely Japanese words and they had learned Japanese nursery rhymes and heard Japanese folktales from their mothers who spoke little English. When they were old enough to attend the public schools, these children became English-speakers and their fluency in Japanese lagged. What if Japanese immigrants and their families were deported? How would their children survive in Japan where they would be as much strangers as their parents were in the United States?

In parts of the West Coast with large populations of ethnic Japanese, such as Los Angeles and San Francisco, U.S. security agents had started quiet surveillance of Japanese American communities well before the war. There is no record of such activity in Colorado, but it is likely authorities were aware of the Denver conference. One can only conjecture that the emphasis on local affairs and their own safety by the Japanese at the conference—who were open enough to stand for a solemn-faced group photograph outside the meeting hall—reassured authorities that they did not pose a security risk. After war broke out, the Federal Bureau of Investigation on the West Coast rounded up hundreds of Issei as a precaution, but only two are known to have been detained in the tri-states area. Ironically, Kano was one of them. (The other was Shiro Toda, publisher of the *Rocky Shimpo* newspaper.) Kano's ties with Japan's aristocracy—and many prominent Japanese who visited him during trips to the United States—may have concerned the FBI.

The bombing of Pearl Harbor on December 7, 1941, launched a wave of fear and apprehension among Colorado's Japanese, and anger and confusion elsewhere. As a consequence, President Franklin D. Roosevelt signed Executive Order 9066 on February 19, 1942, authorizing the military to remove "any or all persons"—including citizens—from areas designated as "sensitive."

The extraordinary fear that led to Executive Order 9066 is reflected in testimony from late February 1942 before a congressional investigative body, the Tolan Committee, by then chief legal officer of California, Attorney General Earl Warren. He said:

> To assume that the enemy has not planned fifth column activities for us in a wave of sabotage is simply to live in a fool's paradise. . . . I am afraid many of our people in other parts of the country are of the opinion that because we have had no sabotage and no fifth column activities in the state since the beginning of the war, that means that none have been planned for us. But I take the view that this is the most ominous sign in our whole situation. It convinces me more than perhaps any other factor that the sabotage that we are to get, the fifth column activities that we are to get, are timed just like Pearl Harbor was timed and just like the invasion of France, and of Denmark, and of Norway, and all those other countries. I believe we are just being lulled into a false sense of security and that the only reason we haven't had disaster in California is because it has been timed for a different date, and that when that time comes if we don't do something about it, it is going to mean disaster both to California and to our nation. Our day of reckoning is bound to come in that regard.*

---

*Warren, who later became the chief justice of the Supreme Court, wrote in his autobiography after retirement that the position he took demanding the ouster or imprisonment of Japanese Americans was one of his most painful mistakes. He and many others believed that because nothing bad had happened after the Pearl Harbor attack, something bad was sure to happen.

The "any or all persons" referred to in Roosevelt's executive order turned out to be all persons of Japanese ancestry, alien and nonalien, and "sensitive areas" eventually encompassed the southern half of Arizona, all of California, the western halves of Oregon and Washington, and all of Alaska. "Non-alien" was obviously a cruel euphemism for citizens who suddenly discovered their constitutional rights had been wiped out by Roosevelt's pen.

For a brief period, all persons of Japanese ancestry in the prohibited areas could move out "voluntarily." This was not easy to do. Where would the evacuees go if they fled from their homes in coastal areas? What would they do with their belongings? How would they support themselves? Some, fortunately, had friends or kin living in interior states, such as Colorado, who they could impose upon. There are no specific figures, but several hundred refugees from the West Coast hurried to Colorado, which in 1940 had an estimated population of no more than 2,000 ethnic Japanese. Most of these evacuees found shelter and jobs with friends or relatives.

Meanwhile, the federal authorities herded all remaining ethnic Japanese in the prohibited zones—some 115,000 of them—into fourteen temporary camps, ringed by barbed wire and hurriedly constructed at fairgrounds and racetracks where there was open space, power, water, and access to sewer lines. These were no more than holding pens for the prisoners until more permanent camps could be built in the interior of the country. Ten of these "relocation centers" were constructed, most of them on desolate federal land. One was in Colorado. It was called Amache and located just outside the town of Granada in the state's sparsely populated southeastern corner. Another was Heart Mountain, between the towns of Cody and Powell in Wyoming's northwestern corner. This camp was to play a significant part in the history of Japanese Americans in Colorado.

In 1943 the War Relocation Authority began a relocation program encouraging the evacuees to leave the camps for jobs in the nation's interior in cities like Chicago, Cleveland, Detroit, Minneapolis, and St. Louis. An estimated 4,000 made their way to Colorado, most of them settling in Denver where the Japanese American population tripled within a few months. They were to leave a deep mark on Colorado.

c h a p t e r   t w o

TODAY:
AN OVERVIEW

To understand contemporary Japanese American life in Colorado, let us begin with the gray granite, gold-domed building—the Colorado state capitol—atop a slope looking out over downtown Denver and to the Rockies on the far western horizon. On the south side of the spacious capitol grounds is a modest monument honoring the memory of Colorado governor Ralph Carr, who played a heroic role in Japanese American history. In a perilous time he risked—and destroyed—his career by taking the then unpopular position that as U.S. citizens Japanese Americans were entitled to all rights guaranteed by the Constitution. He set an example for all Americans to honor.

Enter the capitol building and climb a curving flight of stairs to the second floor. At the north end in what was once the supreme court chambers is a stained-glass window high on the wall. It depicts two Asians—Chinese immigrant Chin Lin Soo and Japanese immigrant Naoichi Hokasono—who were pioneers who helped build the state. An Issei artist, the late Yuri Noda, whose watercolors hang in many Denver homes, designed the Hokasono part of the window.

At the other end of the second floor are the state senate chambers. There a Sansei—a third generation Coloradan—named Stanley Matsunaka as president of the senate directed the course of the state's legislative debate from 2001 to 2003. After serving the two-term limit in the legislature he returned to his home in Loveland to practice law and made two strong but unsuccessful runs for Congress. Another state employee is Ilene Yokoyama-Reed, director of the minority business office in the governor's Office of Economic Development and International Trade.

Not far from the capitol are the Denver Art Museum and Denver's Department of Public Safety, where Art Arita once served as police captain. The museum has a highly regarded collection of Japanese and Asian art, assembled lovingly over three decades by its respected curator, Ronald Otsuka. In a city hall courtroom nearby, municipal judge Melvin Okamoto presides over hearings for citizens in trouble with the law. And across the street, in the offices of the budgeting department in the new Wellington Webb Office Building is Tom Migaki, who served as manager of the Department of General Services in Webb's mayoral administration. Migaki was honored by being named mayor pro tem when Webb traveled to Japan accompanied by Eric Hiraga, then international trade representative in the mayor's Office of Economic Development and International Trade.

Across Colfax Avenue from city hall is another municipal building, a one-time hotel that the city bought to provide offices for expanding departments. Denver renamed the building for the late Minoru Yasui who, as director of the city's Human Relations Com-

A sign of changing times: native Coloradan Stanley Matsunaka being sworn in as president of the Colorado State Senate.

mission in a time of ethnic tensions, helped bring interracial under-standing and tolerance to Denver's multi-ethnic citizenry. In the building's lobby is a bronze bust of Yasui and a wall devoted to re-counting his service to the cause of human rights and the people of Colorado's largest city. Years before any of these Nisei worked for the city, Lloyd Shinsato was assistant city attorney and Colorado na-tive Dr. George Ogura, coroner.

Not far from the civic center, near the banks of Cherry Creek, is the home of Denver's leading television station, KMYR Channel 9, and its star newscaster is a slim, personable Japanese American woman named Adele Arakawa, perennial award-winner. She was preceded at the station by Lori Hirose. And north on Broadway, a few blocks from the capitol, are the offices of the *Denver Post,* the area's largest newspaper, which under an earlier ownership had savaged Japanese

Ronald Otsuka, curator of Asian Art at the Denver Art Museum.

Americans but went on to employ two of them—Bill Hosokawa and Larry Tajiri—in key editorial positions. Currently Kelly Yamanouchi and the Asakawa brothers, Gil and Glen, are on the editorial staff. Several more blocks in the same direction is the new federal courthouse where highly respected magistrate judge Michael Watanabe dispenses justice.

Another bust of Yasui appears alongside busts of Ralph Carr and Rev. Yoshitaka Tamai, a Buddhist priest whose vast contributions to Denver's Japanese American community will be discussed later, at

One of Colorado's best-known faces: Adele Arakawa, award-winning KUSA-TV Channel 9 news anchor.

Sakura Square, an urban renewal project created in a once shabby area. All three busts are the work of Nisei sculptor Tsuyako Kaneko, who also sculpted Yasui's likeness for the city building.

The Denver Buddhist Temple, which occupies one corner of Sakura Square, was responsible for building a controlled-rent apartment tower, a shopping center that includes two restaurants, and a parking garage. Scarcely a day goes by without busloads of elementary schoolchildren visiting the square to gawk at the statues, wander through the Pacific Mercantile store, and listen to a lecture on Buddhism from Rev. Kanya Okamoto, a Sansei veteran of the U.S. Navy.

Decades ago the site of this community center was a slum of shabby stores, cheap restaurants, smoke-filled pool halls, and worse. Now only a long block and a half away is the new Coors Field, home of the Colorado Rockies baseball team.

Denver has enjoyed a warm Sister Cities friendship for more than forty years with Takayama, a Japanese mountain resort city in Gifu Prefecture, close to the Japan Alps. That friendship is symbolized by a Takayama Park in Denver and a Denver Park in Takayama. Although Takayama Park is modest in size and facilities, a more prominent symbol of the Denver-Takayama relationship exists at the Denver Botanic Gardens where a half-acre plot of serenity features a tranquil pond, a teahouse, a stone lantern from Takayama, and other symbols of goodwill.

But significant Japanese American activity in Colorado, both now and in the past, extends beyond Denver. For a quick view, drive north on U.S. Highway 85 to Brighton, headquarters of Sakata Farms. On the way, it is important to make a short detour to visit the vast, green expanse of Fairmount Cemetery, which once adjoined the former Lowry Air Force Base. On the Fairmount grounds is the stark, moving Nisei War Memorial designed by Floyd Tanaka, honoring the nearly fifty Colorado Japanese Americans who died in the service of their country in World War II. Nearby scores of their comrades are buried and the number grows as time speeds by. The rites of remembrance on each Memorial Day find an increasing number of new graves marking the final resting place of the aging Nisei generation.

Brighton is the home of Bob Sakata who was a high school student uprooted by World War II from his father's farm near Oakland, California, when he came to Colorado. Starting with forty acres near Brighton acquired with borrowed money in 1943, Sakata Farms has grown into a year-round operation that now harvests more than three thousand acres of vegetables—sweet corn, cabbage, broccoli, onions—for nationwide distribution. Japanese immigrants, and later their sons, pioneered vegetable farming—where once sugar beets were the primary crop—in the South Platte watershed north from Denver toward Greeley, and from Longmont on the west to Sedgwick in the state's extreme northeast corner. In the inevitable course of events, most of these Japanese farms have disappeared but Sakata, who has been joined by his son Robert, is a notable exception.

Continue north on U.S. 85 to Platteville, home of the late Frank Yamaguchi, a farmer who entered politics and was elected commissioner of Weld County. Drive on to Fort Collins and the campus of Colorado State University where Dr. John Matsushima, a Colorado farm boy, developed a more nutritious feed now used worldwide to put more meat on cattle for less cost.

On the way back to Denver is Longmont where a city park is named for the Kanemoto family whose oldest son, Jim, took over the family farm and became a civic leader after his immigrant father died. Longmont was the center of a variety of early Japanese activities. Japanese Americans had productive truck farms near surrounding towns like Niwot, Lafayette, and Windsor. To the west of Longmont are the high passes of Rocky Mountain National Park where long ago Japanese labor helped build Trail Ridge Road, the scenic highway over the Continental Divide. To the southeast are towns like Erie and Dacono where young Japanese were among the miners working the shallow coal beds. Not far to the south is the University of Colorado where, in World War II, Japanese Americans taught U.S. naval intelligence officers to read, write, and speak the Japanese language. Decades earlier, Japanese farm laborers found winter employment blasting rock for what is now Barker Dam west of Boulder just outside a town called Nederland. No work was too hard. South of Denver they labored in the steel mills in Pueblo and the coal mines near Walsenburg and Trinidad alongside immigrants from Europe.

Some of these Japanese headed eastward along the Arkansas River where around dusty towns like Rocky Ford and Swink and Crowley and Ordway and La Junta they became the backbone of the region's famous cantaloupe and melon industry. And wherever the railroads went—from Sedgwick and Julesburg in Colorado's far northeast to Alamosa in the San Luis Valley to Oak Creek in the northwest—there were likely to be Japanese laborers. A notable exception to these tillers of the soil were the Takakis, a family of dentists in Pueblo. A Sansei son, Dr. Mel, expanded his interests to politics, was elected mayor of Pueblo, and later ran for Congress. Despite an excellent record of dedicated public service that extended statewide, the handicap of being a Republican in a heavily Democratic district was too great. Takaki lost but became something of an elder statesman whose support was sought statewide for good causes. Some years later Mel Takaki left his Pueblo practice and moved to Santa Fe, New Mexico, where he runs a dental clinic for children from indigent families.

The pioneers from Japan are long gone, succeeded by their U.S-born, U.S.-educated offspring, many of whom are now deep into their retirement years. But in recent decades, a few representatives of modern Japan, each with fascinating stories, have found their way here and made their own unique contributions to Colorado. Unlike their largely unschooled predecessors who succeeded by dint of sweat, muscle, and persistence, the new immigrants from Japan are mostly educated men of accomplishment. A few are listed:

- Dr. Kuniaki Hata, retired professor of classical European music and opera at the University of Colorado.

- Dr. Masataka Mizushima, emeritus professor of physics, also at the University of Colorado.

Japanese immigrants usually became farmers. This unidentified cow-
boy was an exception.

- Kitaro, composer of avant-garde music who finds inspiration in the solitude of a mountainside aerie west of Boulder.

- Dr. Akio Suzuki, now retired after managing seed development and marketing in Longmont for Mitsui, the Japanese conglomerate.

- Masa Tanaka, who for many years headed Pentax Camera's operations in the United States, and served on the Denver Symphony Board.

- Michio Morita, associate professor in the electron microscope lab at Colorado State University in Fort Collins.

- Masakazu Ito, classical guitarist, University of Denver.

Additionally, for a number of years, until a series of dry winters damaged the ski industry, a multinational Japanese firm called Kamori Kanko owned and operated the Steamboat Springs ski resort. The Japanese Victoria sports conglomerate owned the now thriving Breckenridge ski resort but left when it ran into hard times. Kaz Sakaguchi, Victoria's first manager, still runs a school in Breckenridge for aspiring Japanese competitive skiers.

Nisei, too, began to move into a variety of professions. Colorado-born Don Tokunaga, a farm boy, worked his way up the ranks of the Federal Bureau of Investigation and became the bureau's director for the state of Washington. Helen Maruyama became a Denver Symphony violinist. Joe Ariki and his wife, Kate, became Denver school principals.

Dr. Roy Sano was appointed bishop of the Rocky Mountain Conference of the United Methodist Church in 1992, then transferred to a similar post in the Los Angeles area. Hank Kashiwa, the Olympics skier, grew up in upper New York state but moved to Denver to start a ski equipment manufacturing company. At this writing Kerry Hada is president-elect of the suburban Arapahoe County Bar Association.

Undoubtedly Colorado's greatest Nisei woman athlete was Nance Ito, who, after an illustrious career in Denver softball leagues, moved to California to play for the Orange Lionettes, a team that won four national championships and was runner-up four times. She was a computer specialist and supervisor for the Federal Aviation Administration for thirty-five years until her death in 1987.

An outstanding Japanese American women athlete of a later era is Longmont-born Kimiko Hirai Soldati whose father, Gary Hirai, was born in the Minidoka (Idaho) internment camp during World War II. Her interest in gymnastics at Longmont High School led her to springboard diving. She has won many awards, including 2002 U.S. Diver of the Year, but her bid for the gold in the three-meter springboard diving event at the 2004 Olympics in Greece was thwarted by a shoulder injury. She is married to Paul Soldati, a diver she met at the University of Indiana.

Today numerous Japanese American physicians, dentists, and attorneys are prominent in the Denver area. Dr. Herbert Maruyama, a transplant from Hawaii, is an orthopedic surgeon who served as president of the Clear Creek Valley Medical Society and has been a member of the Colorado Medical Society's sports medicine committee for fifteen years. His wife, Ruby, is vice president of the executive board of the Colorado Junior Golf Association.

Dr. Ben Miyahara, a microbiologist and his wife Dr. Florence, a specialist at Children's Hospital, after retirement went on Methodist Church medical missions to the Philippines, Venezuela, and Mozambique. After a long career in the Colorado State Department of Revenue, Robert Horiuchi and his wife, Chiyo, went to Afghanistan for two and a half years and to Kenya for two years to help the governments set up revenue and accounting systems.

In more unusual occupations in Colorado are Dana Rikimaru, a trout fishing guide; Mark Konishi, deputy director of the Colorado Division of Wildlife; and Steve Yamashita, assistant regional manager of the Department of Fish and Wildlife in Grand Junction.

Robert Sakata, Bob Sakata's son and partner, is chairman of the Colorado State Water Quality Commission, president of the Colorado Onion Growers Association, and former chairman of the Adams County Open Space Commission.

Leo Goto, owner of one of Denver's premiere restaurants, is a trustee of the University of Denver and chairman of the Colorado State Advisory Committee to the U.S. Civil Rights Commission. James Imatani at one time was a major supplier of cucumbers for national pickle manufacturers. The state's largest supplier of flowers and bedding plants is the Tagawa family. Takeshi Aigaki is a major grower of sod for the lawns of the region's booming homebuilding industry. Denver-born Yutaka Terasaki, only recently deceased, became a pharmacist and was a member of the Colorado State Board of Pharmacy. Lt. Col. Paul Maruyama, who served in Japan, Vietnam, and Thailand, was a member of the U.S. Olympics judo team and former director of the leadership training program for 4,000 cadets at the Air Force Academy near Colorado Springs. Dr. Kathy Sawada, daughter of retired Maj. Ken Sawada who was qualified as a paratrooper, is retired with the rank of captain in the Naval Reserve, a service that until after World War II did not accept Asians except as mess attendants. Electrical contractor Allen Tochihara specializes in huge projects such as installing the lighting for Coors Field in Denver. Ron Abo, president of Abo Copeland Architecture, Inc., and Jim Sato of Sato and Associates are prominent figures in Denver's thriving construction industry. Both firms had significant roles as subcontractors in building Denver International Airport.

THE FIRST VISITORS

The first Japanese to spend any significant amount of time in the United States was a sixteen-year-old castaway fisherman named Nakahama Manjiro. Shipwrecked on a tiny Pacific island, he and several companions were rescued by a U.S. whaling ship called the *John Howland* from New Bedford, Massachussetts. Manjiro's friends were dropped off in Hawaii, but Manjiro went with the captain, William H. Whitfield, to New Bedford where they landed on May 7, 1843. Manjiro was sent to school where he studied English, went to sea where he learned whaling and navigation, and eventually returned in 1852 to his home on Shikoku, the smallest of the main Japanese islands. After Commodore Matthew Calbraith Perry showed up in Japan two years later, Manjiro was summoned to Tokyo (then called Yedo) to serve as an interpreter during the ceremonies establishing relations between the two countries. In 1860 Manjiro was with the first official mission to the United States, which opened the way for a few young Japanese, mostly of noble blood, to come to the United States to study western ways.

By that time Japan should have been well known to literate Coloradans. Denver's first newspaper, the *Rocky Mountain News,* in its first issue, published on April 23, 1859, contained a long story on page one headlined "The Opening of Japan." It reported a treaty with the United States, "granting the fullest privileges," had been "ratified by the Emperor of Japan." The story went on to report that the treaty provided "for the liberty of providing Christian worship and erecting Christian churches in any part of the empire, for the abolition of the annual custom of tramping on the cross that has existed since 1620, and for the extension of religious freedom to all Japanese. These great and unexpected privileges were gained without resort to force or bribery."

The name Colorado was known in Japan as early as 1867 when a ship by that name plied the San Francisco–Yokohama route. The English-language newspaper in Yokohama, the *Weekly Mail,* reported in 1871 that a team made up from members of the *Colorado*'s crew defeated a team of local U.S. civilians in a four-inning baseball game, 15 to 11.

One of the earlier arrivals was twenty-one-year-old Matsudaira Tadaatsu who reportedly came to the United States in 1872, just eighteen years after Commodore Perry opened up Japan to the West and, strangely enough, to Colorado not many years later. Young Matsudaira was born in 1851 at Yedo Castle, which is now part of the Imperial Palace in Tokyo. His father, Tadakata, was one of the four-member Council of Elders that approved the treaty with Perry.

Matsudaira enrolled at Rutgers University in New Brunswick, New Jersey, where several score students from Japan had come to study, and received a degree in engineering in 1878. Reports differ, but apparently he married Cary Sampson the following year in New Jersey and worked in Pennsylvania and other locations before joining Union Pacific Railroad and moving west. He reportedly arrived in Colorado between 1886 and 1888.

Photographs of Matsudaira show a handsome face somewhat longer and thinner than that of the average Japanese and a heavy mustache. One reason Matsudaira may have come to Colorado, after working for a time as a surveyor on the Union Pacific's mainline in Wyoming, was that his father-in-law, William Sampson, had become superintendent of the state reform school in Golden. Before long Matsudaira was appointed assistant to the state inspector of mines.

Matsudaira and Cary had three children: a daughter, Fumiye; a son, Taro, who died in infancy; and a son, Kinjiro, who went on to serve as mayor of Edmonston, a small Maryland town. Matsudaira died in 1888 at age thirty-seven probably from tuberculosis, which at the time was prevalent and had no known cure, and is buried in a remote part of Riverside Cemetery in Denver. His widow apparently returned to Maryland with her two young children. By that time there were an estimated two thousand Japanese living in the United States. Matsudaira was largely forgotten until 1952 when leaders of the Denver Japanese Association raised money for a handsome memorial stone with inscriptions in Japanese and English, the latter inscribed with the following words: "In memory of the first Japanese resident of Colorado." The Matsudaira family is now represented in Colorado by one of Matsudaira's descendants, a grandson named Gary Dent who, although born and raised elsewhere, moved to Colorado as an Air Force officer and now lives in retirement in an isolated mountain valley.

Despite the monument's inscription, there is evidence that other Japanese were in Colorado in Matsudaira's time. (The federal census of 1880 lists no Japanese in Colorado and ten in 1890. How the census-takers arrived at the figure ten is a mystery. The state's population was 194,327 in the 1880 census; by 1890 it had climbed to 413,247.) Kazuo Ito's book *Issei,* a 1,000-page history of Japanese immigrants in North America, which was translated in 1973 by Shinichi Nakamura and Jean S. Gerard, reports:

> As for the mountain regions, the following is recorded:
> "There were definitely a certain number of Japanese, both men and women, in Colorado sometime between 1880 and 1890 before the Japanese Association was formed in Denver. Rumor says that many Japanese female slaves once lived here, but the truth cannot be guaranteed. However, the following tombs were found among weeds at Riverside Cemetery:
> "Infant, Kaku Nakamura died on June 3, 1888.
> "Tadaatsu Matsudaira (brother to Lord Ueda, Nagano Prefecture) died in 1888.
> "Kiku Aoyama, died at 25 on November 16, 1894.
> "One can see small, weather-beaten tombstones bearing only first names (seemingly women with no surnames) buried among Chinese graves. Other than the above, it is recorded at the office that some 30 males and females aged from seventeen to about forty died of fever, consumption, dysentery and other agonies, of suicide and so on. Such tombs of people who had no relatives may be found all over Colorado."

The Kiku Aoyama mentioned above was identified as Kiku Oyama, a nineteen-year-old prostitute, in an article by historian Tom Noel in his *Rocky Mountain News* column of October 23, 2004. Noel wrote that Kiku, who weighed less than 90 pounds, was one of several Japanese prostitutes and a favorite in a high class parlor house at 1957 Market Street. She was found strangled in an alley between Market and Blake Streets. Her assailant was never found. Noel said among her papers were receipts that showed she had been sending $50 a month to her mother in Japan.

In 1888, the same year that Matsudaira died, two Japanese from Kyoto arrived in Colorado to learn something about electric power. Their names were Takagi Bunpei, who would become known as the father of Japan's electric power industry, and Tanabe Sakuro, a twenty-five-year-old engineer. Their visit to Colorado was an afterthought and requires some explanation.

Kyoto, Japan's ancient capital, was suffering from a water shortage at the time. Also, as the distribution center for rice grown in rural provinces on the northwest side of the main island of Honshu, Kyoto needed to be easily accessible to these rural provinces. The existing system for transporting rice was complicated and labor-intensive. Coastal vessels transported rice from northern ports to the town of Tsuruga from where it was moved inland by oxcart to Lake Biwa, Japan's largest lake. The rice was then transported by boat across the lake, reloaded on oxcarts, and hauled over three low ranges of hills to Kyoto on the opposite side of Japan. Takagi was among those who thought there might be an easier way to transport the rice. He proposed building a barge canal from Lake Biwa to Kyoto. The canal would include several tunnels that would have to be drilled through the hills. Drawings from the time show the tunnels were to be about twelve feet across at the base with enough space for oxen or men to haul the barges upstream on the return trip. Thus, the canal would serve the dual purpose of moving freight and providing Kyoto with water.

In one spot near Kyoto, the slope was steep and water flowed too swiftly for the barges to be floated downstream or back up. This problem was solved by building an 1,800-foot-long incline or slide. Each barge was placed on a wheeled cart and gently lowered to the continuation of the canal below the rapids. On the return trip, oxen hauled the barges up the incline.

Two years after the Kyoto project was started, Tanabe saw an article in a U.S. magazine that described an innovative hydroelectric power project near Holyoke, Massachussetts. It said a low dam had been built across a stream and the water diverted into a pelton wheel to generate electric power. Electricity was a new source of energy virtually unknown in Japan, but Tanabe could see how the water flowing through the Kyoto canal might be utilized to produce enough power to haul the barges up the incline. So he and Takagi gained permission to go to the United States to learn more.

Their visit to Massachusetts was disappointing. What they saw could not be adapted to their needs. But there they heard of a revolutionary hydroelectric plant being developed in a faraway mining town called Aspen in the Rocky Mountains west of Denver. After a long, weary train trip they reached Aspen late in 1888 and managed to locate the designer and builder of Colorado's first crude water-powered electric generating plant, a remarkable man named Walter Devereaux. Tanabe quickly recognized that Devereau's system would work for Kyoto. Devereaux helped Tanabe draw up specifications for a plant to be built in Kyoto and they sent off a purchase order for the hardware to General Electric Company in New York. Early in 1889 Tanabe and Takagi sailed for home, and by 1891 Japan's first electric generating plant, designed with the help of a Coloradan, was producing power to lift canal barges and later to illuminate Kyoto's streets and run textile mills. The plant is still in operation and a bronze statue of Tanabe stands next to it.

It was also in 1891 that Nakashima Taizo entered Colorado College in Colorado Springs. Colorado College records report:

He [Nakashima] entered the College as a junior, and spent two years here studying philosophy before graduating with honors in 1893. Although the College has some records of other Japanese attending the College as early as 1885, Dr. Nakashima is the first Japanese student to graduate from Colorado College. Dr. Nakashima displayed a keen interest in the political developments taking place in Japan during the years he was at Colorado College, and eagerly anticipated the future development of Japan as a leading industrialized nation. His stated ambition while at the College was to become a professor of philosophy at a Japanese university. Dr. Nakashima delivered a speech at his commencement entitled "The Modern Movement Against Metaphysics," in which he argued that the scientific method was successfully encroaching upon the territory of metaphysics.

In an article in *The Colorado Collegian* magazine Nakashima wrote, "We Japanese young men feel, today, the necessity of establishing what we may designate 'a Japanese Christian church.'" He went on to say, "We Japanese young men are very willing to accept Christianity in the sense in which we believe it to have existed in 'the mind of Christ' and will endeavor to undermine one by one, those props on which have rested those unsightly and repulsive additions built up by the perverted ingenuity of theologians around the original edifice."

None of this is likely to have resonated with other Japanese who in this period had begun to come to Colorado to supplement Chinese labor—whose numbers were dwindling as a result of the Chinese Exclusion Act in 1882—and compete with southern European immigrants for jobs in the mines, mills, and railroads. Much of what follows is based on a remarkably detailed study undertaken by a Japanese student, Fumio Ozawa, working on a thesis for his master's degree at the University of Denver in the 1950s. His thesis is part of a book titled "Japanese American Who's Who," published by the *Colorado Times* in 1959 with a preface by Minoru Yasui.

Ozawa's findings can be summarized in six paragraphs from the abstract of his study:

> The principal cause of the Japanese coming to Colorado was almost entirely economic, and involved the expansion of Japanese activities eastward from the Pacific Coast, the expansion of the railroads of the West, and the rapid growth of the Colorado economy.
>
> Most of the Japanese came to Colorado as common laborers, railroad workers, miners, farm hands, factory workers and domestics.

Reared on tiny rice farms in their native country, Japanese immigrants adapted quickly to American farm practices.

The largest segment of those workers was composed of farm hands who concentrated along the South Platte and Arkansas Rivers in sugar beet fields.

The largest number of Japanese came to Colorado during 1903–1908.

The relations between the Japanese and the other races in Colorado were better than those in the Pacific Coast, because the Japanese population in the state was small, and most of them were farm hands who were in great demand. The failure of the Japanese and Korean Exclusion Leagues of Colorado was due to the fact that the formation of the Leagues was the product of labor movements and was not supported by public opinion.

Success or failure of Japanese settlement in this country depended greatly upon the environment which surrounded the newcomers. Courteous treatment and consideration for their needs and welfare appear to have produced good results.

Understandably, this summary does not capture the drama, the heartache, the blood, sweat, and tears of these sojourners.

chapter four

WORKIN' ON THE RAILROAD

By 1900 the vast reaches of Colorado were stitched together by hundreds of miles of railroad crossing the prairies; taking supplies into the mountains and bringing out the ore; linking ranches with meat packers in Omaha, Kansas City, and Chicago; and coming back with manufactured goods.

The rails had to be maintained and new lines constructed as the frontier advanced. At first the Irish, and later the Chinese and immigrants from southern Europe and Mexico, provided the labor. In 1882 Congress, under pressure from West Coast labor leaders who felt threatened by Asian workers, passed the Chinese Exclusion Act sealing off that source of labor. But southern European workers were often inclined to be difficult to manage and the railroads turned to Japanese immigrants for help. They worked hard and worked for less than whites. Equally important, they had a "boss" system under which

The first job for Japanese immigrants in Colorado was with railroad section crews who rode handcars from bunkhouses to work sites.

contractors took the responsibility of hiring and maintaining crews of laborers for the railroads.

The most enterprising among the Japanese immigrants became labor contractors. Japanese author Hisashi Tsurutani in his book *America Bound* reports that Kyutaro Abiko, who founded the *Japanese American News* in San Francisco in 1899, established the Japanese-American Labor Contract Company in 1903 to supply Japanese laborers to railroads, mines, and farms in several states including Utah. To recruit young Japanese farm boys to work on the Great Northern Railroad and the Northern Pacific in Montana, Ototaka Yamaoka, Tetsuo Takahashi, and Matajiro Tsukuno established the Oriental Trading Company in Seattle. Tsutomu Wakimoto and Ryuun Nishimura formed the Wakimoto-Nishimura Company in 1902, which supplied the Union Pacific with hundreds of Japanese laborers in Wyoming. In one document Wakimoto claimed in 1906 that he was supplying Union Pacific with two thousand workers, although this number has been disputed. Terasaburo Kuranaga recruited workers for the Union Pacific in the central mountain areas. Shinzaburo Ban started a general merchandise store in Portland, Oregon, in 1902 and soon expanded into railroad labor contracting. Four years later he set up branch offices in Sheridan, Wyoming, and in Denver through which he operated a dry goods store, distributed Japanese provisions throughout the state, and also provided labor for the Burlington Railroad in Colorado and Wyoming.

But the big man in Colorado was Naoichi (Harry) Hokasono. Born in Oita Province, he came to the United States in 1893 at age twenty. Five years later he opened a restaurant in Denver and by 1903 he was a general labor contractor—building roads and dams, stringing power lines, as well as maintaining railroads—with Japanese workers in Colorado and Wyoming. Because of his contributions, he is commemorated, as mentioned earlier, in the Colorado state capitol.

The railroad laborers, called section hands, were hired to keep up the tracks as well as construct new lines. And later a few Japanese were employed in the roundhouses where locomotives received routine maintenance. For most of this era the railroads paid the contractors $1.10 to $1.25 a day for each workman, and the contractors paid the men $0.95 to a dollar with the contractors providing food and housing. Usually the section hands were housed in remodeled old freight cars that were parked on some isolated siding. The nearest water, aside from a limited supply delivered for drinking and cooking, was likely to be a stream or pond. The food the contractors supplied was mostly flour, which the designated cook managed to convert into an inexpensive stew called *dango-jiru* in Japanese (*dango* meaning "dumpling" and *jiru* meaning "soup") and flavored with a few slices of bacon. This was the main item, and with this unbalanced diet the malnourished men often suffered from night-blindness. Occasionally a chicken bought, bartered, or stolen from a nearby farmer and greens plucked in season from a field added variety to the *dango-jiru*. One oft-repeated story tells of a Japanese section hand who sought to buy eggs from a white farmer. Trying to make the farmer understand, the Japanese squatted on the ground, flapped his arms, made a cackling noise, and dropped an egg-sized stone. He got his eggs.

It was understandable that the laborers looked forward to any opportunity to go to town—Denver in the case of workers in eastern Colorado—and spent much of their meager earnings for some decent food, a hot bath, and entertainment, which usually including whoring and gambling. One source says Denver's Japanese population about this time was no more than 800. In his thesis, Fumio Ozawa says the 1910 federal census recorded only 585 Japanese in Denver and 2,300 throughout Colorado. But anti-Japanese sentiment had begun to appear because they were perceived as strike-breakers and competition on the farms.

The situation in Colorado was not as bad as in California. In 1907 the Fresno Federated Trades and Labor Council in California passed a resolution that said:

> Whereas the Japanese in this country have by their arrogant and insulting manners become a menace to the best interests of good society, and
>
> Whereas the merchants of this city, knowing full well that this class of people are a detriment to the community . . . therefore be it
>
> Resolved that we, the delegates to the Federated Trades and Labor Council of Fresno, in regular session assembled, do pledge

Welcome to America! A sight familiar to Japanese immigrants.

ourselves not to patronize any place of business where there is employed a Japanese, and further be it

Resolved, that we request the affiliated unions of this council to endorse our action in this matter, and that they be further requested to make it part of their by-laws, "That to patronize a place of business wherein there is employed a Japanese will be a violation of the trade rules of their respective unions."

Employ none but White Labor and the Japanese question will solve itself. These undesirable people, finding themselves without employment in America, will return to their own country.

This attitude was prevalent in other communities and thus Issei, and Nisei as well, were barred from unions controlling various crafts like carpentry, plumbing, or brick-laying. So it was inevitable that immigrants would seek work in the hard, unskilled, and undesirable occupations. Perhaps anticipating growing problems for the Issei in Colorado, Hokasono imported printing type from Japan and published a small pamphlet that has been translated as follows:

> At this time the White Union has formed the Japanese Exclusion Association in order to expel us from Colorado, like our compatriots were in San Francisco and other regions. This is indeed the most critical time for not only Japanese residing in the State of Colorado but all those in the intermountain region as well. Therefore, each and every one of us, as Japanese, should behave discreetly to avoid dishonoring the Yamato race, while striving to obtain the sympathy of honest and decent Americans. We should minimize the criticisms about us by heeding the following items, even if they appear trivial in nature:
>
> 1. Do not patronize gambling houses, brothels, and other immoral establishments.
> 2. When in public, hold yourself upright and do not talk or laugh too loudly.
> 3. Do not frequent or loiter en masse in dangerous or crowded places.
> 4. Do not appear intoxicated in public or create any disruptive scenes.
> 5. Hotel and restaurant owners should close their doors by 11 P.M. Do not disturb our neighbors, or interrupt their sleep, by loud singing or playing musical instruments like the *shamisen* late at night.
> 6. Do not make hostile gestures toward Whites.
> 7. Do not draw unwanted attention to yourself from Whites by appearing unkempt or carrying soiled items.
> 9. Never carry pistols or knives.
> 10. Always carry a whistle for emergencies.

Denver's Japanese population during this period never exceeded one thousand, but Bureau of Labor statistics show that in August, September, and October 1907, money orders sent to Japan from one Denver post office amounted to $14,987, and $8,655 from another post office. Because Japanese laborers were being paid about a dollar a day, such remittances to families back home indicate that the Japanese population might have been larger and that most of their earnings were being saved and sent back home.

At the time six or seven small hotels or rooming houses were in Denver's Japantown centered around Twentieth and Larimer Streets. There were as many as three bathhouses (which may have been no more than ordinary bathtubs with a supply of hot water), several barber shops and pool halls, and a store selling a limited supply of Japanese groceries. Ito's book reports that public bathhouses run by Japanese in Seattle during the period charged 15 to 25 cents depending on the facilities, and presumably that was the going rate in Denver.

One of the few public voices protesting the anti-Japanese agitation was the now defunct *Denver Republican* newspaper, which quoted a Japanese student identified only as Saito: "I do not think there is any reason the laboring men here should wish to drive out my countrymen. There are not enough Japanese here to take away their jobs. Most of my people are doing domestic work, cleaning houses, waiting on table and cooking. Most of the Japanese that are seen here just come into town for a few days, then go out on farms to work, or back to the railroads." This undoubtedly was true, but there is no indication that anyone paid attention to Saito's earnest plea for understanding.

chapter   f i v e

COAL AND STEEL

Not iron ore but gold and silver were the minerals that first attracted settlers to the Colorado mountains in the second half of the eighteenth century, and the Chinese began to arrive toward the end of the precious metals boom. Many of them were former employees of the Central Pacific Railroad and had lost their jobs when it joined rails with the Union Pacific at Promontory, Utah, on May 10, 1869, completing the first transcontinental line.

In Colorado their first jobs usually were in labor gangs shoveling gravel into the sluice boxes of placer mines in the rarified air of Gilpin and Park Counties. This was an unattractive labor-intensive occupation avoided by other workers. William Wei, professor of history at the University of Colorado, has written that these Chinese worked six or seven days a week for about $35 a month without board. If they wished to mine independently, about the only way the Chinese could expect to share the wealth was as scavengers picking over abandoned tailings. The Chinese Exclusion Act of 1882 halted Chinese immigration and by the time the Japanese began to arrive, there were only a handful of Chinese in Denver.

Like the Chinese, many Japanese entered the U.S. labor market through railroad jobs and other occupations demanding men who—because they were unskilled and did not know English—would work hard for little pay. An important entry point into the labor market in the nation's interior was coal mining, an industry not well known in Japan and one that required little more than a strong back and a willingness to work underground. Hisashi Tsurutani in his book *America Bound* reports that starting around 1900 West Coast labor contractors began sending Japanese to work in the mines around Rock Springs and Kemmerer, Wyoming. One report says that around 1910 about 2,000 Japanese were working in the Kemmerer area, but this number might have included Japanese workers in all of western Wyoming.

Inevitably some of these men drifted down into Colorado where they found work not only on the railroads but in coal mines south of Walsenberg and north of Denver, steel mills of Pueblo, and farms Japanese immigrants were developing in the valleys of the South Platte and Arkansas Rivers.

The direct reason for Japanese entry into Colorado mines was the growing strength of the United Mine Workers Union. Work in the mines was punishing; the pay, marginal. The miners, mostly immigrants from southern Europe, were willing to listen to union organizers' promises of more pay and better conditions, and the prospect of higher operating costs worried mine owners. To put it bluntly, the Japanese were sought as potential strikebreakers.

Ozawa writes in his thesis, "Whatever the truthful reason may have been for the importation of the Japanese miners, the fact remains that the Japanese remained in the coal fields of Southern Colorado, despite the opposition of the labor unions, because the coal mines in these districts were under the control of the big mine companies such as the Colorado Fuel and Iron Co., the Victor Fuel Co., and the Union Pacific Fuel Co., and effective labor union organizations did not exist."

Many Japanese preferred the mining jobs in northern Colorado, where the union was less well organized because of the proximity to Denver's attractions. The late Dr. Thomas Kobayashi recalled that his parents made a living operating rooming houses for northern Colorado miners. In the north, coal was relatively close to the surface so these mines played out fairly quickly; therefore, the coal companies would move from one location to the next, followed by the miners and the Kobayashi family.

These were rough and violent times. One source reports that two Japanese were among the twenty fatalities in the Ludlow Massacre south of Pueblo in which Colorado troops fired into an encampment of strikers and their families. Nothing has been found to confirm this story; however, while researching his book *America Bound,* Hisashi Tsurutani found references to several nameless individuals identified only as "A Jap" in Wyoming coronors' records of mine accident victims.

Just as Japanese immigrants in Utah worked in the copper smelters not far from Salt Lake City, scores of Japanese were employed in the Colorado Fuel and Iron steel mill in Pueblo. They may have been inexperienced in steel-making, but they soon learned the craft of tending blast furnaces, rolling rails and sheets from molten steel, and stretching wire. But this was hard, hot, and grimy work and the Japanese were happy to leave the mill at the first opportunity and try farming in the nearby Arkansas Valley where many prospered.

Among the most successful was Sadakichi Harada, who in time was shipping cantaloupe and onions, processed in his own sheds, to eastern markets under the S. Harada Farms label. His sons Shige, Mitsu, and Uji carried on the business while son Henry went to New Mexico to launch his own operation. Colorado's growing demand for water, however, crippled farming in the area. Cities on the Rockies' eastern slope—primarily Pueblo, Colorado Springs, and Aurora—have bought up water rights in the Arkansas River drainage and many once prosperous farms in that area have reverted to grazing land.

As many Japanese Americans moved westward from the Arkansas Valley over the Continental Divide to the San Luis Valley, at least one sought his fortune in the other direction. Barry Shioshita, who grew up in the Sierra Grande area of the San Luis Valley and graduated from Adams State College in Alamosa, is the highly regarded commissioner—the chief administrative officer—of Otero County whose seat is in La Junta in the Arkansas Valley. In 2003 the Association of Colorado County Administrators named him county administrator of the year.

chapter six

ONE MAN'S STORY

Much of the story of early Japanese immigration to the United
States is from long-ago recollections of aging immigrants. But this
chapter is based on the diary of a Coloradan who faithfully kept a
journal of his thoughts and activities in the early years of the last
century.

That man was Shingo Nakamura. In 1906 he left Itojima, his
village in Fukuoka Prefecture on Kyushu, the southernmost of the
main Japanese islands, to go to Mexico. He wanted to come to the
United States but he could not get an immigration permit. So he
settled for Mexico and eventually made his way to the United States
and Colorado.

After faithfully keeping a journal for many years, Nakamura simply
put his journal away as he grew older. He died in 1978, at age ninety,
in California. His journal, neatly written in Japanese and illustrated

with rough sketches, was given by his daughter, Masa Nishimura of Denver, to Simpson United Methodist Church in Arvada because she could not read Japanese and did not know what to do with the material. For years the journal remained largely unnoticed among the scores of books in the ministers' library. Then one day Nakamura's writing came to the attention of Rev. Yukio Yamasaki, a minister from Japan who was on assignment at Simpson to serve the Japanese-speaking members of the congregation. It was quickly apparent to the minister that the journal contained a wealth of fascinating information for Nakamura's descendants as well as all Japanese Americans, almost none of whom knew enough of the ancestral language to read the memoirs.

Yamasaki mentioned the journals to his friend, Minoru Mochizuki, a San Francisco–born Nisei and Presbyterian minister retired in Denver after a long career in Michigan. Unlike most Nisei, Mochizuki was fluent in Japanese. The two clergymen obtained Masa Nishimura's permission to translate the diaries, and for the next six months they spent one afternoon a week on the self-imposed assignment. They completed work on just one volume before Yamasaki was recalled to Japan, and work on the other volumes has not been resumed. The translation they completed, however, is a manuscript of forty-nine typewritten pages, single-spaced, and is the basis for this chapter.

Nakamura wrote that food was scarce in Japan in 1906 after the Russo-Japanese War. Some of his friends in his village were migrating to America in search of jobs, but he understood it was difficult to get permission to enter the United States. About that time he read some pamphlets·about opportunities to be found in Mexico working in the sugarcane fields. Without much further thought he applied to the Fukuoka prefectural government for permission to go.

In October 1906 he received notice from the Fukuoka authorities giving him permission to go abroad and ordering him to report to get his documents. The documents included instructions about his behavior as a citizen from Fukuoka, and some of those he remembered were the following:

- Do not break the customs of the land.
- As a Japanese citizen, do not do anything that would embarrass us.
- Obey the laws of the land and work diligently.
- Do not forget that you came from Fukuoka.

Early in December 1906, he boarded a coastal ship at the port of Moji to go to Kobe where he would take another ship to cross the Pacific. Nakamura wrote in his journal that he began to hear unpleasant reports about life in Mexico from others on board and he thought about returning home, but once he reached Kobe he realized he could not change his mind. After a two-day stay at an inn, he boarded a China Line ship for the thirteen-day voyage across the Pacific with more than a hundred other young Japanese, half of whom were bound for San Francisco and the others for Mexico, all packed into the fetid steerage area.

"When we got to San Francisco," Nishimura wrote in his journal,

50 or 60 of us going on to Mexico were confined on board ship. Rihichi and his brother [not otherwise identified] were the first to jump ship in San Francisco. They left about 11 P.M. Following them, Narumi and Inaba also jumped ship. They used a rope to get down from the ship. Nakamata was loaded down with his luggage and apparently he had eaten much too much. As he was trying to get down on the rope, he lost his grip and fell into the water. When he hit water, it made a loud noise and that stirred a

lot of commotion. We began to hear the voices of the police. We on board just buried our heads deeper into our blankets. The Coast Guard came quickly with their boats and Nakamata was caught. After that we were stopped from even going up onto the upper deck.

Several days later the approximately sixty men bound for Mexico were put aboard another ship that sailed south along the California coast. Nakamura wrote in his journal: "As we sailed south, I gazed longingly at the mountainous landscape of California. I felt apprehensive about what lay ahead. I realized that we were passing by a land of fruits and vegetables and many Japanese working and living there. I cried as I wondered whether I would ever be able to live in such a place. We stopped in Mazatlan. The morning fog was thick and silent."

The ship stopped at one small port after another on the southward journey as the days grew hotter. After a week it arrived at a place called Buena Vista where the Japanese disembarked. Nakamura does not identify the area other than to say the cane fields, run by a company he called Oaxakenia, were close to the ocean. He wrote in his journal: "Unfortunately it was not a place where humans could live. The word circulated that all the Japanese who had gotten to Mexico with an earlier group had escaped to America. I prepared myself to live rather than die in such a place. If I were lucky, I would end up in America; if not I imagined myself dying in Mexico." Nakamura's contract was for two years.

It was the living conditions, rather than the hard labor of the cane fields, that bothered the Japanese most. He wrote in his journal:

Mosquitos were horrible all the time. Every Sunday we got into the routine of going to the ocean. We went to bathe and to wash our clothes. The Mexicans warned us about crocodiles in the deeper parts of the river. We were told that the black snakes were safe but all the others were poisonous. What we suffered most when the heavy rains came was that we had no drinking water because the runoff made the river muddy red. It would take three days to prepare such water for consumption. . . .

We were working under a contract where we were free to leave after two years. We worked 10 hours a day. Our meals cost 25 cents, beer was 5 cents and a kilo of meat cost 65 cents. Our savings amounted to 25 cents. The labor company took 25 cents per day and we were told that were we to run away, they would return nothing. There was no doctor, no medicines, no hospital, no school, no church, no police. It took mail two and a half months to get to Japan.

When we worked out in the fields harvesting cane, a white man would come out to the field about three in the afternoon every day and check on what we had done. Each of us had a card which would show the amount of sugar cane we had cut. That white man would tell us, "You are too slow," or "You have been eating too much sugar cane," and would dock us a half day's pay.

To get from where we worked to Mexico City, it took a train overnight. Then to get to the border of the United States, it was a four-night, five-day train trip. Anybody who wanted to get on the train would stand on the tracks and wave.

When Nakamura had completed his contract, the sugar company took him by wagon to the railroad station for the overnight trip to Mexico City. There, he wrote in his journal, he boarded another train for the long ride through mostly desert country to the U.S. border. "I didn't see any houses along the way," he recalled years later.

In another part of his journal, however, he writes about walking ten days to two weeks along the railroad tracks to get to the United States. "We suffered a great deal from the lack of water," he wrote. "There were just a few trains coming by and certainly there were almost no people living in the desert." Unfortunately, Nakamura does not reveal in his journal how he was able to cross the border, why he chose to go to Denver, and how he finally reached his destination. We do know that he soon met other Japanese in Denver and was sent, possibly by labor contractor Hokasono, to work on farms near Atwood in northeastern Colorado not far from the town of Sterling.

On the 13th of September, Nakamura wrote in his journal,

frost had already come. I went to pick beans at the farm of a *hakujin* [white person]. I picked all day and earned $1.30. Little though it was, I was glad to have had a job and that I was able to get paid for it.

One evening, when the stars were out, the temperature was so cold that the leaves of the sugar beets wilted. About the 23rd of the month we started to harvest sugar beets. We Japanese were the work crew, three or four of us pulling up and topping the beets. Then the *hakujin* crew pitched the beets on to a horse-driven wagon and drove it to the railroad station to be moved to the sugar processing plant. We worked at an intense pace. I'm sure no one in Japan would be able to see men working at such a pace.

At the beginning of November the beet harvest ended so we took off for Denver. I had earned $300. After paying off some debts and buying winter clothes, I was still able to send $50 home to Japan. Our hotel was in the Chinese section of Denver. The Chinese gambling houses were full of Japanese men. I paid 10 cents for a bath, had a beer and *udon* noodles, and paid 5 cents for a movie. With these activities I was content and went back to the hotel.

Next day I decided to work at the hydroelectric power construction project up in the Rockies.

Although Nakamura does not specify, he probably went to Hokasono's labor contracting office to sign up for work on what came to be known as the Barker Dam near Nederland, west of Boulder, being built for the Public Service Company. "I went to the Golden Eagle store," Nakamura wrote, "bought two of the cheapest comforters, and borrowed a couple of blankets." He took the Rio Grande train to Lyons and was met by a Mr. Toyobe in a horse-drawn cart for the trip up the mountains to the Japanese camp. "As we drove," Nakamura wrote, "it was so cold that my feet almost froze. I was also very hungry. We got to the camp at about 4 P.M. He didn't seem to be in any hurry."

The workers apparently rested and ate in a building heated by a large wood-burning stove but slept in tents that provided little protection against the mountain cold. "We pitched our tents where the wind was least severe," Nakamura said in his journal.

> We laid the floor with green pine boughs and we laid a blanket on top of that.
>
> The work place was nearby. There were about 200 men in our work gang, divided into groups of about five men. Each day we lugged dynamite up the mountain. The sounds of the dynamite blasts were very loud. After the blasts we cleared the debris by hand. There were two Japanese who died in accidents.

In May, when finally spring returned to the Rockies, Nakamura went back to Atwood. Beet seed had been planted, and soon the shoots would have to be thinned with short-handled hoes, a tedious, backbreaking job. He felt at home in Atwood and wrote in his journal, "I began to think that as long as a person was willing to work hard, he could make money in America."

After the thinning period (which the Japanese pronounced "shinning"), there was little to do until the fall harvest. Nakamura and three of his friends worked with a railroad section gang between Brush and Hillrose nearby, then moved on to Sidney, Nebraska, to work on the railroad for a month and a half before returning to Atwood for the beet harvest. He wrote: "We found the work quite manageable. I began to think that this was the life of working America."

When the harvest ended Nakamura decided to spend the oncoming winter again in the damsite camp. "It was the same as the year before," he wrote.

> We pitched our tent in the snow. One night we really had a heavy snowfall. It was so heavy our tent collapsed on us and we had to take shelter in our neighbor's tent.
>
> Our work every day was the same. We bored holes in the rock to place the dynamite. After we blew the rocks apart, we would cart the broken rock away. We were able to make $2.50 a day. We had *sake* [Japanese wine] morning and night. Sunday was rest day. Fellows from other work sites would come to visit. We would talk about girls, particularly about Omasu, the lovely Japanese prostitute in Denver.

Not every man, however, was an itinerant laborer. Take the case of Fred Kawamura, who drifted into Colorado from Wyoming. Not satisfied with ordinary work, he learned mechanics and built and raced cars. He saved enough money to go to flight school and get his pilot's license. Finally, he married at age forty-two, settled down to run an auto repair shop in Denver, and raised ten children.

In spring 1912, four years after Nakamura had come to Denver, he and three friends each put up $250 to try their hands at farming. They rented sixty acres near Merino in Logan County near Atwood, which they knew so well; borrowed money from the bank to buy six horses; and rented farm equipment to plant alfalfa and sugar beets. "The crops were neither good nor bad," Nakamura wrote. "Two of the partners were married and their wives didn't take to farm life so they decided to quit the partnership. Although we had contracted

Fred Kawamura, who was issued a pilot's license in 1921, made his living at an automobile repair shop in Denver.

the land for only a year, Ishida [not otherwise identified] and I agreed to pick up the responsibility of farming together."

They were hoping for an opportunity to rent a better farm when they received word from a Mr. Ono, farming near Iliff, twenty-eight miles from Atwood, who said there was property for rent nearby. Nakamura wrote, "We promptly got on the 3 o'clock train and went to Sterling. Then we walked the 10 or so miles to Iliff. What we went to check out was a 360-acre property. The next day we agreed on the lease; 360 acres is a lot of land so we agreed to have Mr. Kuronaka who lived nearby to farm 60 of the acres."

"Even though we worked very hard," Nakamura wrote, "we were novices and did poorly. One day Ishida went to town and ran into an American who said he had a 180-acre farm not far from Iliff, with a good supply of water, that he wanted to rent. Ishida and I decided to take a chance."

The land they rented had never been cultivated. "Our first beet harvest was the best that I had seen," Nakamura wrote. "We had ample water and we worked hard. That year I borrowed another 160 acres north of Sterling and we put it into wheat."

Farming brought a measure of stability into Nakamura's life. When he first arrived in northeastern Colorado, lumberyards were almost nonexistent and many farmers lived in soddies—holes dug into the ground with turf (sod) built up as walls and roof. But within a few years a lumberyard was opened in a town seventeen roadless miles from Nakamura's farm. It took him three days to make the round trip to town and back with a wagonload of lumber, with which he built a small but comfortable home on the prairie. Now that he had a decent place to live, he noted with some envy that other men were returning to Japan and bringing brides back to the United States.

The wheat crop in 1916 proved to be unusually good. Nakamura paid off his bank loan and had enough money to go home to Japan for the first time in ten years and perhaps find a wife who would agree to go back to America with him. He went to Seattle and joined a group of about fifty men "who, like me, were going to Japan to look for a wife." They set sail on December 23, 1916. During the boring voyage Nakamura wrote several poems to express his joy about what he was setting out to do. In rough translation, his poems follow:

Ten years ago I came east. I entered the port of San Francisco.
This time I am going West.
It is the same ocean but it is now carrying me home.
Though we 50 [men] have separate hopes and plans,
We share the same ocean; we share the same feelings.

*Not an uncommon sight on Colorado's dryland farms. While Mama worked else-
where in the fields, Papa was plowman and took his turn as baby-sitter.*

> I recalled a lot of my past,
> But today I rejoice at what lies ahead.
> I join my hands in prayer
> And with that joy, I rejoice with the 50 on board.

On landing at Yokohama the travelers checked into an inn and
indulged in a few days of sightseeing around Tokyo, an area they had
never seen because most were country boys who had not left home
until they sailed for the United States. Nakamura wrote another poem.

> Oh, God of Japan, I have landed on your soil.
> I have come to offer you my prayer.
> My tears won't stop because I am so happy.

Nakamura finally arrived home on January 16, 1917, to a tearful
welcome from his mother and numerous relatives. The next day they
visited the family shrine to pray for the souls of departed kin, and
afterward there was much feasting.

Oddly enough, he wrote not a word about meeting the woman he was to marry. Apparently it had been arranged before Nakamura ever reached home. Her name was Kichi, and that is all we know about her. We do not know what she was like or what Nakamura's feelings were when he first met her. We know only that the go-betweens who arranged the match were Matsuura Zenji and his wife.

Nakamura wrote in his journal:

Early in February, mother, my brother and I went to the town of Fukuhiro to buy clothing for my wedding. Feb. 26, 1917 was the day of my wedding, a day I surely cannot forget.

Since it gets pretty busy on the farm in March, we got ready to leave for home. We said our good-byes to our family and friends. We left Hakata at 1 P.M. on the Tsubame limited express train for Moji.

He does not provide the date that he returned to the United States. Apparently it was only a few days after the wedding. Nor does he say anything about his bride's feelings about heading for a new life in a new land.

They took a ship heading for Vancouver, British Columbia, and finally reached the Colorado town of Sterling, the railroad stop closest to Nakamura's farm, on April 26, 1917. Nakamura's journal provides no hint about his bride's reactions on seeing her humble new home on the endless Colorado plains.

The years passed and Nakamura's family grew until there were eight children, more American than Japanese. Somehow he survived the terrible economic times of the Great Depression—there was little market for his crops and no money to repay the bank loan he had taken out to lease more property. "I am unable to write about the misery and agony of that period," he confided in his journal. But he continued to note such developments as hiring three white men to

Shingo Nakamura slipped across the Mexican border and came to Colorado in
1908. He returned to Japan in 1916 and brought his bride, Kichi, to Colorado in
1917. This family photo was taken in 1946. Back row, left to right: Tsuru Thelma
Bell, Amy Kurihara (deceased), Masa Nishimura, Mike (deceased). Front row:
Barbara Harr, Mama Kichi, Suzie Toshiko Davis, Papa Shingo, Hideko Beverly
Kurihara.

help harvest his beet crop in 1935 because his children were still too
young to be of much help.

In the late 1930s the economy had begun to improve, but now
he worried about growing tension between the United States and his
homeland as Japan invaded Manchuria and gave every indication of
further aggression. "Now we Japanese had to face the possibility of
war between America and Japan," he wrote in his journal. "An announcement calling for a meeting in Denver of Japanese residing in
Colorado, Wyoming and Nebraska was issued."

As president of the Japanese Farmers Association in northeastern Colorado, Nakamura attended this meeting. "More than a hundred men gathered to discuss what might be done in the light of a possibility of such a war," he wrote.

> That meeting allowed each of us to express what we thought about the various ways we might handle ourselves if such an emergency were to occur. Some expressed the thought of fleeing to Mexico. Others talked of protecting themselves by arming themselves. There were some who said that since their children were American citizens, they had the right to defend themselves with firearms in the event that they were attacked.
>
> We tried to make our thoughts known to the government— that we were willing to do what the government asked of us. The thought that all of us shared was that if one person caused a problem by violating the government's decrees, it would affect all the rest of us. Everyone needs to be careful to obey the government. With that kind of warning, the meeting concluded.

Nakamura felt an obligation to lead the Japanese in his area and circulated some guidelines for their behavior. As he wrote in his journal, he urged, "We should stop all gambling. All members of the Association should take a half day off on Sundays and start attending church along with the *hakujins* [white people]. I encourage each family to help their children continue their education beyond high school and on to college. Make a yearly contribution to the *hakujin* church. However, at home you need to continue using the Japanese language with your family."

Nakamura's son Mike heard the news of the attack on Pearl Harbor on December 7 and alerted the family. Nakamura had to attend a wedding, but apparently no one there knew about the war's outbreak. "I thought it best not to discuss what had happened in Hawaii," he wrote.

"But we were quite anxious for our safety. We managed to get through Sterling without any trouble and got back home safely. I couldn't sleep very well that night, wondering what might happen to us."

Early on December 8, the day after the Pearl Harbor attack, the pastor of their church visited the Nakamura home. Nakamura wrote in his journal, "He said a terrible thing has happened. He went on to tell me that if other *hakujin* were to cause trouble for us, he and his congregation would be ready to journey together with us. Furthermore, he continued, we at the church are prepared to take care of you and provide for your daily needs."

The next day a representative of the sugar refinery came to tell Nakamura that under government edict the company could not pay enemy aliens for the beets they had delivered. "Without the $50 I was owed," Nakamura wrote, "I was unable to pay my workers." Ironically, the Colorado state agriculture department urged farmers to produce more food. "They even made bank loans easy to get," Nakamura noted.

Some weeks after war's outbreak, as demands on the West Coast grew for the ouster of all Japanese, Nakamura received a letter from an old friend in California, Kofuyo Matsuura. He asked if he and his family of seven could stay with the Nakamuras if they had to leave their home. Nakamura hurried into town to ask an attorney what he could do to help his friend.

The next day a federal government official showed up at the Nakamura home to ask about his farm and his willingness to take in the California family. "I told him I farmed 225 acres," Nakamura wrote. "I told him we had 25 head of cattle we were feeding, five horses, three tractors, two trucks and two cars for family use. As for the cultivated fields, 65 acres were in sugar beets, 50 acres in wheat, 40 acres in corn and I had a plot for growing vegetables. And I told him I would take responsibility for the Matsuura family."

Shingo Nakamura and his wife, Kichi, on their fiftieth wedding anniversary.

Not long afterward the seven Matsuuras, jammed into their car with a few belongings, arrived at the Nakamura home. "Our house was quite full," Nakamura reported. "Meal times, especially, were cheerful times." But he also wrote, "My heart was heavy and gloomy at what was happening around us. As a result of the distrust that I sensed, we tried to live unobtrusively. We lived quietly and made sure that we went to church service every Sunday."

Gradually the situation improved. Nakamura observed, "Since we had interacted with our neighbors for many years, we began to see each other as people who live in the same community. Among those people were a goodly number who had Italian and German ancestry. I took the attitude that we all worked under the Stars and Stripes, and therefore we were no different from the others nor they from me."

But not everyone agreed. Nakamura's son Mike was studying at Colorado State University to be a teacher and was assigned as a student instructor in Sterling, not far from Iliff. After a few days some parents demanded that the school get rid of the "enemy" teacher. University officials bowed to the protests but gave Mike credit for a full term of student teaching.

Shingo Nakamura died in 1978 at age ninety. His heirs sold the farm. None of his children had any interest in farming, except perhaps Masa who married John Nishimura, a native Coloradan and soil chemist with the federal Department of Agriculture.

chapter seven

ADOPTING CHRISTIANITY

In stories of the old Wild West, a Christian clergyman is often in the background urging the rough frontiersmen to reject temptation and sin, worship God, and live clean lives. But in the earliest years of Japanese immigration to Colorado, the unattached young Japanese, as Buddhists, had nowhere to turn for spiritual guidance even if they had wished for it.

It did not take long, however, for Christians to seek converts among the Japanese. Early in 1907 in Pueblo Rev. G. F. Porter, a Methodist, sought to reach out to the young Japanese in the nearby steel mills and coal mines. He quickly found language a difficult barrier. He wrote to Methodist missionaries in Japan, told them of his need, and asked for a native Japanese minister to be sent to Colorado. Rev. Hachiro Shirato arrived in August to work among Japanese in Pueblo and elsewhere in Colorado, Wyoming, and Nebraska.

In September of that same year Hamanosuke Shigeta, a Denver layman and devout Christian* who owned a small restaurant invited some friends to talk about founding a Christian church. Two men showed up. They met in a building in the 2100 block of Arapahoe Street. That is said to be the beginning of the California Street Methodist Church, now Simpson United Methodist Church in the Denver suburb of Arvada.

By January 1908, Shigeta had drummed up enough support to bring out eighty persons, Japanese and Caucasian, to another meeting with Shirato also in attendance. By June the organizers felt confident enough to ask for membership in the Japanese Methodist Episcopal Mission, headed by Dr. Herbert B. Johnson, in California. Shirato was appointed pastor of both Denver and Pueblo area churches. A year after acceptance the Denver church took up residence at 1827 Park Avenue. During this period Mrs. Shirato organized the San-to (East of the Mountains) Fujinkai, or Ladies Aid Society.

A booklet published by Simpson United Methodist Church in 1984 reports:

Apparently there was significant interest in Christian ideals among Japanese in Denver in 1908, as the Presiding Elder of the Methodist Church reported that "Two hundred and fifty Japanese in the city met to welcome me and to hear me speak." He further observed, "There are in and about Denver about one thousand Japanese, many of them representing a very desirable class. The conversion of a few hundred, or even tens, will mean much to the uplifting of Japanese society there in Denver."

Despite this optimism the work went slowly. At the close of 1909 the tiny church reported a membership of three with a Sunday school enrollment of 10. By 1912 the congregation had

*It is not known how or why Hamanosuke Shigeta converted to Christianity.

grown to 25 (still small but representing a 700 percent increase) and 25 Sunday schoolers.

By December 1914 the congregation was large enough to take over the historic St. James Methodist Church building on West Colfax Avenue from a congregation that had outgrown it. A dedication service on Christmas Day was attended by more than two hundred.

Shirato was assisted during this period by Revs. Sadao Nakanishi and Iwataro Arauchi, and Junzo Sasamori, a University of Denver graduate student in political science from Japan, who had been baptized in 1901. When Shirato returned to Japan in 1916, Sasamori was named acting minister. After completing his studies, Sasamori also went home to Japan. In later years he was elected to parliament, served as cabinet minister, and was considered a special friend among Denver Japanese.

In 1919 the St. James building suffered heavy fire damage and the congregation moved to 2801 Curtis Street, which was a combination parsonage and church with services held in the living and dining rooms. These modest quarters were sufficient for a decade and a half. Then, a church history reports, "In 1935 the board of trustees voted to purchase the German Congregation building at 25th and California. This is the first church that many present day Simpson parishioners remember."

At that time the name was changed to California Street Methodist Episcopal Church. The pastor was the deeply respected Rev. Seijiro Uemura, who was in the middle of his eighteen-year Denver ministry, which spanned the period between the Great Depression and World War II. One of his most faithful supporters was an Issei named Masaichi Otsuki, whose wife Todome helped make the church more than a religious center by promoting a variety of Japanese cultural activities.

Acquisition of the new church building added impetus to the Young People's Christian Conference, which had its uncertain beginnings in 1930 when older Japanese Americans began to realize the need for interaction among young people of Japanese ancestry. Despite the "Christian" in its name, within a few years it was drawing to Denver as many as three hundred Nisei—including Buddhists and those of no religious affiliation. These participants came from Colorado communities such as Greeley, Sterling, Rocky Ford, Las Animas, Pueblo, Alamosa, and later Wyoming and Nebraska each Thanksgiving weekend for socializing and discussion of mutual problems. The church history says, "It was the all-inclusive gathering for young people of Japanese ancestry in this area and was a great opportunity to get acquainted. . . . The Uemura family was the guiding light for this gathering."

Gradually the California Street congregation grew as increasing numbers of Nisei reached maturity. During the war years the church and many parishioners opened their doors and offered their resources to support displaced families—those driven from the West Coast by federal order. The congregation, one report notes, "pulled together in the face of racial prejudice and still supported their young men in the armed forces during this confusing time."

Postwar it became evident the congregation was outgrowing the California Street church. Sunday school classes were overflowing. Parking was inadequate around the church. The church leadership started a building fund and looked for available church buildings outgrown by other congregations.

Meanwhile, another church, Simpson Methodist at Thirty-fourth and High Streets with an all-white membership, was having problems of another kind. This area's character was changing. One history reports, "The congregation dwindled as many residents left the increasingly interracial neighborhood for the suburbs. The social phenomenon known as 'white flight' left Simpson with as few as 28 persons at services and finally no minister."

Simpson Methodist was named for Bishop Matthew Simpson, an early clergyman reputed to have been a friend of Abraham Lincoln, and had been founded on Denver's Market Street in 1882. When the building burned, the sixteen members worshipped in tents until they built a new church at Thirty-seventh and Lafayette Streets in 1889. In 1908 the congregation moved into the church at Thirty-fourth and High Streets.*

Dr. Bruce McDivitt, head of the Methodist Denver district at the time, is credited with suggesting the then astonishing proposal to merge the white Simpson and the ethnic Japanese California Street congregations. On September 12, 1960, the board of the California Street church held an emergency meeting and decided to inspect the Simpson church and consider the possibility of a merger. That same day Simpson officially closed its doors after members indicated they would like to join the California Street congregation. A church history notes, "Were Simpson members fearful of strangers assuming leadership and bringing in a relatively large membership? 'No,' asserts Dale Ritter, a board member and today a valued member of the (new) Simpson Church. 'We welcomed them . . . we liked the ministers, and we needed help paying the bills.'"

On October 9, 1960, the first service of the newly joined congregations was conducted by the two California Street pastors, Rev. Paul Hagiya and Rev. Jonathan Fujita. It was hailed as "a unique experiment in Christian brotherhood." Shortly afterward the cumbersome

---

*High street has now been renamed Bruce Randolph Avenue in honor of a much-loved black barbecue restaurant owner and, reflecting the area's changing demographics, the building is occupied by Epworth UMC–Iglesia Metodista.

Simpson–California Street Methodist Church" name was changed to simply "Simpson Methodist Church." Many thought it peculiar that a Japanese name was not selected, but the members saw nothing wrong with honoring Bishop Simpson.

By the early 1960s, even the new church building rapidly was becoming too small for its growing congregation. As more and more Nisei established families, Sunday school enrollment exceeded three hundred.

The story of how the church was able to build and move into a new building is a well-remembered part of Simpson history. One day in 1964, the story goes, Hagiya, a World War II veteran and Simpson's English-language pastor, was in his office praying for guidance as he sought a solution to his church's crowding problems.* His prayers were interrupted by a telephone call from one of the church's most active members, Vi Otsuki Nishimura. After some preliminaries, she explained that she and her husband, Roy, had inherited a modest piece of land in suburban Arvada where her father, Motoichi Otsuki, an early and devout Christian, had grown strawberries. Then she asked whether Simpson would be interested in accepting a gift of an acre of that land "way out in Arvada" from her family as the site for a new church. It is church legend that Hagiya cried in shock and elation: "The Lord has truly heard and answered our prayers."

Such an offer was staggering, but there were questions. Would Japanese Americans families, who now lived in all parts of the Denver metropolitan area, continue to support a church in a distant northwestern suburb? And what about the cost of constructing a new building? Ultimately, it was decided to go for it.

---

*The Reverend Mr. Hagiya served from 1959 to 1974, and his energetic, well-loved Japanese-speaking partner from 1959 to 1970 was the Reverend Jonathan Fujita.

A pledge drive with a goal of $150,000 was launched. In two weeks pledges totaled $210,000. With these pledges as collateral, Key Savings and Loan (whose management included Methodists) provided a construction loan of $148,000 at 6.5 percent interest. Later, the Nishimuras donated an additional half acre when the church purchased adjoining land for a parking lot. Groundbreaking services were held on Palm Sunday, April 3, 1966. The first service in the new building was held July 30, 1967. The total cost was $367,000, which was paid off in twelve years. A mortgage-burning service was held in November 1976. Costs were reduced by church members who undertook simple tasks such as painting the basement.

Today Simpson, whose architecture includes touches reminiscent of a Japanese temple, is the center for a variety of activities ranging from the traditional fund-raising bazaar to annual sale of peaches from Colorado's Western Slope, from Japanese cultural programs to a bridge club. And as the Japanese American population ages, it is the site for frequent funeral services. Racial integration has continued. The congregation has been favored by a series of dynamic ministers, among them Rev. Nobuko Miyake-Stoner who was born a Buddhist in Japan but as a young adult came to the United States on her own to enroll in a seminary. Her dedication and service to the Simpson congregation has been recognized by the Rocky Mountain Conference, which appointed her superintendent of churches in the Denver area. As this is written the English-speaking pastor is Rev. Mark Heiss and, since Yamasaki's return to Japan, there is no fulltime Japanese-speaking minister. The church, however, is having financial problems as many of its younger members drop out or join congregations in areas where they live. In 2005 the church reluctantly eliminated the position of youth pastor, which had been held by a California-born Yonsei, Wendi Kamori Stager.

chapter eight

THE BUDDHISTS

Formalized Buddhism in Colorado can be traced back to the arrival of Rev. Tessho Ono from San Francisco in 1916. The year before, he and two other priests had visited Pueblo, Rocky Ford, Denver, Brighton, Fort Lupton, and other areas where Japanese had settled and had found a great yearning among them for a priest who could provide spiritual guidance and conduct traditional services. The decision was made to establish a presence in Colorado, and Ono came to Denver and was feted at a happy welcome party on March 13 of the following year. Two days later his hosts organized committees in various parts of Colorado to raise funds for leasing a building in Denver to serve as a temple.

Rev. Kanya Okamoto, now head priest, explains the importance of the temple: "In Japan a person by law had to be registered with a local temple at birth, so nominally every Issei was a Buddhist. In the streets of Denver an Issei could be called Jap or Chink, but at the temple—where they felt at home—they were human beings. The Issei felt at peace. The temple offered the immigrants a safe place, spiritually and culturally."

On April 16 the leaders rented the People's Tabernacle on Lawrence Street for the Denver Buddhist Temple's first service. Some 250 persons attended. It was called the largest gathering up to that time in the history of the Denver Japanese community. On Memorial Day six weeks later, services were held in memory of the approximately one hundred Japanese whose names were recorded—but whose graves were not always identified—at Riverside Cemetery.

Meanwhile, Ono was busy establishing Kyudokai (support groups) wherever there were settlements of Japanese immigrants, including places like Pueblo, Fort Lupton, Brighton, Henderson and Wattenburg, Eaton and Ault. The priest made his rounds by train or motorcycle; an automobile was considered too costly because income for the first six months was only $1,063.35 with expenditures of $1,204.55. By summer 1917 the temple, in modest rented quarters at 1917 Market Street, could claim membership of some 850 full and supporting members although this most likely included members of the Kyudokai from all over the state.

Two years later the members were optimistic enough about the future to agree to buy the more spacious but notorious "House of Mirrors," a one-time establishment of ill repute, at 1942 Market Street for $10,000. That seemed to be an attractive price until, a few years later, they discovered that the building would require about $15,000 worth of repairs. The temple remained at this site until 1947.

In spring 1929 Ono was succeeded by an energetic younger man, Rev. Yoshinao Ouchi. In 1930, Buddhism in Colorado entered a new era when a stocky, smiling young man named Yoshitaka Tamai,

The Denver Buddhist Temple seen from Lawrence Street, with Tamai Tower low-rent housing project in background.

with virtually no experience in the priesthood, arrived as assistant to Ouchi. Born October 10, 1900, in Toyama-ken on the largely rural west side of Japan's main island, Tamai had majored in philosophy at Toyo University, completing postgraduate studies in 1926. After four years in the editorial department of the Kodansha Magazine Company in Tokyo, he came to Denver.

How he happened to be assigned to Denver is not known. He knew nothing about America and had never headed a temple. He must have been staggered by what he found. One of the first problems he discovered was that the temple's finances were in deplorable shape. He was to be paid $60 per month but there was no money in the bank to cover his paycheck. If he was shocked that the temple was housed in a rickety old building where the notorious Mattie Silks had conducted a thriving business in commercialized sin, it was the least of his worries. The temple was three months' behind on mortgage and utility payments and the roof was badly in need of repairs. Indeed, one night the ceiling of his room collapsed under the weight of the water that had leaked through the roof. The debts totaled $6,000. Soon Ouchi asked for reassignment because he could not support his three children on his salary, leaving the younger priest in charge. Tamai figured if the temple was worth saving, it was worth sacrificing for. He offered to forgo $1,000 of his salary if the directors would raise the other $5,000.

Within a month's time the directors, going from house to house in Denver's Japanese community, were able to raise the $5,000, and Tamai's $1,000 pledge was deducted from his pay over a two-year period. The leaky roof was soon repaired and, after he was named head priest, Tamai launched a career of long and distinguished service to the community, which ended thirty-two years later in 1964 when he relinquished the title of chief priest to Rev. Shodo Tsunoda.

Realizing that young Nisei men in some rural areas outside Denver were not getting the education they deserved, Tamai established a dormitory for as many as twenty in the upper floors of Mattie's former place of business and invited parents to send their sons to Denver for schooling. During the day they attended classes at Manual High School; in the evening they studied the Japanese language and Buddhist scriptures and kept in shape with kendo drills.

Meanwhile, Tamai was busy taking Buddhism, like a circuit rider, to Japanese farm families in outlying areas where, despite a limited population, groups of Japanese were organizing modest facilities for practicing their faith. His trips to the San Luis Valley were as long as three hundred miles each way, much of it over high mountain roads—an arduous venture for cars of the day. Invariably older Nisei were pressed into service as his drivers.

Nobuo Furuiye, one of his drivers, remembered the priest's refusal to see bad in anything. On one trip, he recalled, their car suffered a flat tire at night on a lonely gravel road high in the mountains. When Furuiye muttered darkly about their bad luck, the priest said, "Nobuo, you must understand we are very fortunate. The tire went flat, but the car suffered no other damage. We were not hurt. We did not collide with another car. We did no damage to others. The moon is out so that you can see to change the tire. We are fortunate to have a spare. We must give thanks."

At their destination, whether it might be in far southwestern Colorado, Rocky Ford in the Arkansas Valley, or the farm towns along the Platte River in northeastern Colorado, the Denver visitors depended upon the hospitality of local Japanese families for food and shelter.

In Tamai's later years much of the traveling responsibilities were taken over by Tsunoda, the temple's first completely bilingual priest. Early in 1944, when newcomers from the camps were changing the makeup of Colorado's Japanese population, the leaders of the Denver Temple saw the need for an English-speaking priest to assist Tamai. They found him in the person of the Santa Barbara–born Tsunoda, then in the Poston camp in Arizona. Tsunoda had studied at Ryukoku University in Japan and both he and his wife, Mutsuyo, were fluent in Japanese and English. They came to Denver in late summer 1944. Mrs. Tsunoda, who served the temple as Sunday school and cultural programs leader, died in 1973 and a chapel was built in her memory. Tsunoda retired after thirty years of service and died in 2005.

In the Longmont-Lafayette area north of Denver, Japanese farmers as early as 1925 had established the Longmont Kyudokai, holding its organizational meeting at the farm home of Kikutaro Mayeda. The founding members were Mayeda, Kunihei Miyasaki, Daijiro Furuiye, Motozo Matsuda, Seizo Fukaye, Goroku Kanemoto,

Toyokichi Kawano, and Kamekichi Shimoda, and there were about twenty families in all. After four years they erected a two-room building north of Lafayette where the priest from Denver came once a month to conduct services.

In contrast to the hardscrabble times experienced by other Buddhist congregations, the Longmont temple fared well thanks to the generosity of the Jim and George Kanemoto families. When the Kanemotos donated ten acres to the city for a new elementary school in the early 1960s, the school board gave them the old brick schoolhouse on a knoll at the south end of the city. The Kanemotos then donated the building to the members of the Longmont and Lafayette congregation to serve as their new temple. The members sold their old hall north of Lafayette and the proceeds were used to renovate the schoolhouse into an attractive temple that was dedicated in August 1968.

In the 1920s Buddhists in the Alamosa–La Jara area in the San Luis Valley of southwestern Colorado were also talking about building a temple, but it took them a while to get started. In 1936, despite the dark clouds of a national economic depression, the twelve members of the Alamosa–La Jara Kyudokai—there were approximately two hundred Japanese in the entire area—announced plans to build the Buddhist Church of La Jara. Y. Hattori was named chairman and Roy Inouye, a Nisei, secretary.

Indicative of the friends the Japanese had made in the valley, much of their support came from Caucasians. A property owner named L. A. Braiden offered to sell a site in the town of La Jara for $100, then decided to donate the property, accepting payment of one dollar to meet legal requirements. According to an article by Dr. Morris C. Cohen in the *San Luis Valley Historian,* the publication of the San Luis Valley Historical Society, a total of $4,000 was raised for the building fund, and of that sum $1,188.19 was contributed by Caucasians. Their donations ranged from $50 to 25 cents, and the most unusual gift was a quarter ton of coal. W. W. Platt, an Alamosa attorney, handled the legal work without charge. When an additional $800 was needed to complete the interior, the sum was borrowed from the First National Bank of La Jara. Dr. Cohen's account adds:

> Plans for the new church were sketched by Mr. Miller, manager of the Conejos Lumber Co., in pencil on a piece of plain brown paper. Roy Davis, the contractor, worked from this. Construction began in October 1936 after the foundation was prepared by the Kyudokai members. . . . It took about 20 days to complete the temple. . . . Working weekends and evenings, the Buddhists completed the interior of the church. This took several weeks because it was harvest time and the men were busy in the fields.
>
> By February 1937 all was in readiness for the long awaited temple dedication. Great preparations were made; a group was chosen to visit the Fort Lupton Kyudokai to learn correct procedures. . . . All Buddhist organizations in the state have been invited to be present and it is definitely known that Buddhists from Brighton, Rocky Ford, Fort Lupton, Blanca, San Acacio and Alamosa will attend.

But times change. "In 1993," Dr. Cohen reported, "there are only about six families and a few single members who belong to the La Jara Buddhist church. The Buddhist reverend still comes from Denver once a month to hold services."*

---

*The story of Japanese Americans in the San Luis Valley is remarkable in another way. In the 1920s, when anti-alien laws prohibited land ownership by Japanese immigrants in California and elsewhere, the Gibson Land Company, which owned vast acreages in the valley, sent representatives to the West Coast to invite Japanese farmers to come to Colorado. What happened as a result will be told in Chapter 12.

Today the Denver Temple, through the person of Okamoto, continues its association with Buddhist congregations around the state. Born in the Gila River WRA camp during the war to a Nisei mother and an Issei father, Okamoto considers himself a Sansei. In his early boyhood the family moved to Los Angeles where he grew up under the influence of the Senshin Buddhist Temple near the University of Southern California. After graduation from high school in 1961 he served in the U.S. Navy for three years just before the Vietnam War was heating up, studied under the G.I. Bill, and went to Japan to qualify for the priesthood. He came to Denver in 1975 for his first assignment. The congregation had never known a priest like Okamoto Sensei. He could take part in judo drills or conduct a service, play basketball with the kids or officiate at a funeral. In addition to his duties in Denver he makes monthly visits to Buddhist congregations in Brighton, Fort Lupton, Greeley, Longmont, Sedgewick, and Alamosa; makes calls in Rocky Ford; and occasionally drives to Scottsbluff, Nebraska. The temple has provided him with six automobiles in twenty-eight years and each has rolled up 130,000 to 150,000 miles. Currently his bilingual associate from Japan is a young priest named Kazuya Iino.

By 1947 the Buddhist congregation in Denver, reinforced by a number of Japanese families who had moved to Colorado during the war, was able to abandon its Market Street facilities and build a more fitting temple on a Lawrence Street lot that Dr. Eizo Hayano had bought years earlier for $4,300 and held for the temple if it should ever need it. Back in 1940 the congregation had considered building a temple on the site, but several factors blocked the idea. Agricultural prices were still low following the Depression, and contributions from farmers could not be counted on. Relations between Japan and the United States seemed to be worsening and the future was unclear. But by 1947, with a Denver Japanese population more than double the prewar numbers, the time was right to build a more fitting temple.

It was a tan brick building on Lawrence Street between Nineteenth and Twentieth Streets with a chapel that could be used as a community hall and was named the Tri-State Buddhist Temple. The temple cost approximately $150,000, which by then the congregation could fund with the help of various Kyodokai.

By 1957 it was the consensus that the chapel should be used only for religious services, and an adjoining auditorium was needed for community activities. Two years later an auditorium and a large social room were added to the building—and later a gymnasium—which have become the center of community activities.

Two years after the first expansion, tragedy struck. A fire, probably touched off by an electrical short, destroyed the elaborately crafted altar area where the priests performed their rites, and smoke damage was extensive through much of the rest of the building. Reconstruction would be very expensive. But there were other considerations. There had been discussion of expanding the temple's activities to include care of the growing number of the elderly, perhaps a low-rent housing facility under temple auspices. And there had been reports that before long the entire area around the temple would be razed by an ambitious Federal Urban Renewal project to revitalize a rundown section close to downtown Denver.

The temple's financial problems had been eased somewhat by the generosity of Dr. Eizo Hayano who put up his own property as security in 1959 to help the temple buy the Kenney Hotel for $92,500 as an investment. Seven years later it was sold for $127,000. The profit was used to establish an endowment fund that Ed Nakagawa managed for more than thirty-five years.

The late Reverend Yoshitaka Tamai, beloved Buddhist priest.

But first things first. The congregation raised funds to install an impressively beautiful new altar in 1964 to replace the one that had been damaged in the fire. What followed is the multi-million dollar Sakura Square project, including commercial space and an apartment tower for the elderly, that transformed an important part of Denver's

Lower Downtown section. How the members of the Tri-State Buddhist Church made possible this most significant development will be told in another chapter.

Tamai died September 25, 1983, just short of his eighty-third birthday. In his memory the Institute of Buddhist Studies in Berkeley, California, established the Tamai Professorial Chair, which has an endowment of more than one million dollars and is contributed to by his admirers from all over the nation.

A few years before his death Tamai said in an interview, "We must not think of the Buddhist Temple as a place for social gatherings. Instead, it should be a place where we can feel *Shinjin*—Faith. Jodo Shinshu will prosper in America because, in spite of the fact that America is a prosperous country, human sufferings and anguish will never cease."

Meanwhile, the makeup of the temple's membership was changing. The Denver Buddhist Temple is no longer an exclusively Japanese institution. As many as one-third of the members, according to Okamoto's estimation, are Caucasians some of whom, without being proselytized, have become interested in Buddhist philosophy and attend temple services. Others are multi-ethnic spouses of Japanese American Buddhists who have become interested in the faith. In early 2004 the temple sponsored a series of classes to study Buddhism and its relation to Hinduism. The instructor was Dr. Ginni Ishimatsu, a Japanese American who is associate professor of religious studies at the University of Denver. The Denver Buddhist Temple, once the spiritual home of Japanese immigrants, has become multi-ethnic—just as have the descendants of those Japanese immigrants.

chapter nine

THE ASSOCIATIONS

It has been said that when two Chinese get together in America, they open a restaurant. It also might be said that when two or more Japanese get together, they organize an association for mutual benefit and protection. Unfortunately they don't seem to keep good records.

The Japanese scholar Fumio Ozawa, quoted earlier in this book, reports that the first association of Japanese in Colorado was formed in 1907: "The Association, which had a membership of 639 in 1909, was organized in 1907 when the anti-Japanese feeling grew stronger among the labor unions. When the Japanese and Korean Exclusion League was organized in Colorado in 1908, the quick action of this association prevented the serious development of anti-Japanese sentiment. The first president of this organization was Takesuke Okubo, who was also the president of the boarding and lodging house keepers' association."

However, Eiichi Imada, editor and publisher of the postwar weekly newspaper *Rocky Mountain Jiho,* has reported a slightly different version. He has written that the Japanese Committee of Colorado was founded in 1908 with Tomajiro Kawamoto as its first president. Succeeding him as president, Imada writes, were "Takesuke Okubo, Bunji Tokunaga, Naoichi Hokasono, Bujinosuke Kashiwano. In 1917 they changed the organization's name to Santoh Nihonjin-kai, and united Colorado, Wyoming and New Mexico through a delegate system. The first president was Toichiro Ichikawa, followed by Kakutaro Nakagawa, Bunji Tokunaga, Dr. Konai Miyamoto and Dr. Eizo Hayano. In 1934 the association changed the name again to Colorado Shu Nihonjin-Kai, meaning Japanese Association of the State of Colorado, and exercised jurisdiction only over Denver and its surrounding area."

Nineteen thirty-four was also the year the association purchased a building at 2109 Lawrence Street for use as its offices and a community center. Officers at the time were Dr. Miyamoto, president; Jingoro Kuroki, vice-president; Tomihachi Kawano and Fusakichi Takamine, treasurers. The decision to buy the building was wise financially, but it led to a curious and not entirely distressing problem that persists to this day.

Despite the difficult economic times, some 260 individual contributions were made to buy the building, an old two-story structure that had been a private home. "A gift to the Nisei and future generations from the Issei," many said as they donated their hard-earned dollars. The building was dilapidated and it took many months of volunteer labor to renovate it. Various individuals contributed tables and chairs and other furnishings. In May 1935 Japanese language classes were started in the building for some forty young Nisei. Because no funds were available for paying teachers, University of Denver students George Uyemura and Toshiro Tsubokawa, later to return to Colorado as newspaper publisher, volunteered. The second floor was used as an assembly hall for meetings and celebrations and a place where men could come for cards and board games.

Although in describing the association Imada uses the phrase "exercised jurisdiction," it had no real authority except to try and look after the welfare of Japanese residents. Gradually most of its activity was in the area of social services. The ill and destitute were taken care of locally if they had no families, or helped to go home to Japan. The dead were buried with proper rites. Except for three years, the Japanese Association served as a surrogate for the Japanese Consulate in San Francisco, filing the necessary reports about community activities. Dr. Albert L. Bennett, an English-born American and physician who had visited the Far East, served as honorary Japanese consul general between 1909 and 1912. Infrequently some one from the consulate in San Francisco would come to Denver on an inspection tour, and officers of the association would entertain him.

Other than limited social services and celebration of New Year's banquets and the emperor's birthday, there had been little significant activity by the association until growing tension between the United States and Japan led to the early 1941 Denver conference of Japanese leaders from communities in Colorado, Nebraska, and Wyoming (described in Chapter 1).

Postwar, as Denver's Japanese population drifted away from the city center, use of the building diminished. By 1960 the building, elderly to begin with, seemed to require constant maintenance and the area around Twenty-first and Lawrence was changing from residential to light industrial and commercial. Should the association try to sell the property? Or, out of sentiment, should it spend a lot of money it didn't have to restore it? Time passed without action until one day in summer 1982.

Colorado at the time was enjoying an oil boom. The demand for petroleum led to extensive exploration of fields in Wyoming and Montana by companies headquartered in Denver. There were rosy hopes for development of oil shale deposits in western Colorado. New buildings were erected in downtown Denver to house oil and engineering companies and law firms. Premium prices were paid for building sites.

During that summer a real estate broker notified the Japanese Association that a Canadian firm, East-West Investment Partners, was interested in purchasing their property. The character of the area was changing and obviously would continue to change. A huge urban renewal project, which would engulf the traditional Japantown area, had reached Twentieth Street within a block of the association's property. Investors were looking for sites that could be bought and held for future development.

The association's president, Henry Suzuki, summoned the board for a series of meetings. Suzuki's vice-presidents were Shizuo Yamada, Frank Uyenishi, Mitsutaro Miyahara, Sadako Tsubokawa, and John Hanatani. Minoru Yasui was the association's attorney. Some Issei members urged that the building be kept as a token of respect for local Japanese history. They argued that it had been purchased at considerable sacrifice to serve the community and it should be retained for use as a retirement home. But younger members pointed out that the building would require extensive repairs if it were to be kept, and because the offer—amounting to close to $380,000—was huge in relation to what the building had cost years earlier, it should be sold.

Eventually the decision was made to sell the property, with key Issei members agreeing only with the understanding that the association would reinvest the money in a building to serve as its office, and that the association also would build a retirement home.

With Minoru Yasui as its attorney, the contract was signed on September 1, 1982. The sale price was $376,651.80 with a down payment of $93,149.05. The balance of some $282,000 was to be paid off within five years. Meanwhile, interest payments were to be made on the unpaid balance.

A little more than two years later the Japanese Association formed an Office Building and Retirement Home Construction Committee to make plans for acquiring replacement property. Its members were Nobuo Furuiye, Motoichi Ozaki, Kazuo Yamasaki, Yoshito Tsuchimoto, Mrs. Sadako Tsubokawa, and Harry Aoyagi. Three months later the committee reported back with discouraging news. Suitable buildings were virtually nonexistent; the buildings they had examined were too expensive or in undesirable locations. And founding and operating a retirement home posed monumental problems.

In October 1985 the association received even more shocking news. East-West Investment Partners had declared bankruptcy. The Japanese Association reclaimed the property and retained the down payment, but the building was gone. It had been demolished by East-West in anticipation of developing the property. The association had received payments of some $93,000 and now it had an empty lot. The oil boom was fading. (Fortunately, in later years the association has realized some income from the property by leasing it as a parking lot after the Colorado Rockies major league baseball team built Coors Field, a huge new ballpark, close by.)

Now the association had to face the problem of what to do with the forfeited money from the sale gone awry. Some members insisted the association still had an obligation to build or buy an office building and provide the community with a retirement home. Others contended that undertaking such a program had become unrealistic and beyond the association's abilities and that the resources should be used to support other worthy programs in the community.

Generally, opinion was separated by a generational line. The founders of the association—foreign-born, traditional, and harboring a sense of ownership—were disappearing. They were being replaced by members of the American-born generation with ideas quite different from those of their elders. Additionally, there was an influx of young Japanese immigrants who had not applied for U.S. citizenship and had joined the association and whose outlook was more Japanese than American. A letter written on February 21, 1989, by one of the Nisei members, Kent Yoritomo, put the problem in perspective. It said in part:

> [I]t is time that we should seriously examine the goals and objectives of the Association and a preliminary step in that direction would be to update the constitution and by-laws of the organization. It is clear that the current membership is advancing in age and that younger Japanese Americans are not joining the Association in significant numbers. Also the number of Japanese nationals in the Denver metropolitan area is increasing and the projections are that that trend will continue. Furthermore, it is becoming more apparent that their perspective of what the Association is and what it should do is markedly different from that of the current membership. Thus, if you have any ideas on what direction the Association should take or not take, then you should express those views through the constitution and by-laws.

The Japanese Association of Colorado, in by-laws dated October 15, 1983, states its purposes as follows:

> To foster American ideals of democracy and the practices of good citizenship; to uphold the Constitution of the United States of America and the Constitution of the State of Colorado; to strive

for the elimination of prejudice, ignorance and discrimination because of race, color, creed, ancestry or parentage; to promote the cultural heritage of Japanese Americans in the United States and in Colorado; to enhance the image and status of persons of Japanese American background; to provide for the welfare and well-being of persons of Japanese ancestry; to promote active participation in civic and national life; and to secure justice, equal opportunity and equal treatment of persons of Japanese ancestry in the United States, and particularly in the State of Colorado, as well as for all Americans, to the end that all people can live in peace and harmony in their respective communities.

The fine hand of Minoru Yasui, the volunteer attorney for the association, is visible in this statement of purpose. Yasui, like most Nisei, was a strong advocate of the integration of Japanese Americans into American society and he envisioned a leadership role for the association in this direction.

Five years after adopting the by-laws, and a few months after Kent Yoritomo wrote his letter quoted earlier, the association revised the sections titled "Goals and Objectives" as follows:

GOALS: To improve and maintain the general welfare of the peoples of Japanese ancestry in the State of Colorado so that they can participate more fully in American society without losing their unique identity and shall be secure in their daily lives.

OBJECTIVES: To protect the rights of the peoples of Japanese ancestry in the State of Colorado. To provide mutual assistance among peoples and organizations and maintain the welfare of the Nikkei community in Colorado. To promote respect for and recognition of the rich cultural heritage and unique identity of the Japanese people among the general public. To develop and project a more positive image of the Japanese people and to uphold the public image of high morality. To promote goodwill and friendship between the countries of Japan and the United States and their peoples.

The return to emphasizing the "Japanese" aspects of the association's concerns upset some Nisei members. Then president Tom Masamori, a veteran of U.S. Army service in World War II, member of the American Legion, and a JACL stalwart, resigned saying he could not serve an organization so thoroughly Japanese. So Nobuo Furuiye, a Colorado native and also a decorated veteran of U.S. military service, took over.

The list of association presidents since 1945 reflects its changing nature. From 1945, when World War II ended, until 1985, the presidents were Dr. Konai Miyamoto, Seishiro Nakamura, Yutaka Inai, and Eijiro Kawamura—all born and reared in Japan. Since then the presidents, listed in order of service, were Henry Suzuki and Frank Torizawa, both born as Japanese but naturalized residents of the United States since youth; Tom Masamori, Nobuo Furuiye, Mrs. Sadako Tsubokawa, Seiji Tanaka, James Terada (the last three born in Japan but longtime residents of the United States), and Nisei Jim Shinbara and Jim Hada. Mrs. Kimiko Side, serving her second term as association president as this is written, came to the United States from Japan as a war bride, acquired U.S. citizenship, and quickly threw herself into community and international activities. She was succeeded by Hada, Colorado-born and also an Army veteran.

Today the association is largely a community social service organization. It contributes generously to the Japanese American Community Scholarship program. It has given to both the Simpson Methodist Church and the Denver Buddhist Temple and looks to the comfort of the elderly in retirement homes and Tamai Tower. It sends flowers to the ailing and *koden* monetary funeral offerings to the bereaved. It sponsors New Year's entertainment programs for the community

The altar at Arvada's Simpson United Methodist Church, which has a multiracial congregation.

and it contributed $7,500 to the National Japanese American Memorial in Washington, D.C., a compromise figure reached only after debate as to whether the donation should be $5,000 or $10,000. And a handsome sum of money remains in the bank.

Despite its stated objectives, the "Americanization" of the Japanese Association was highly visible at its 2004 New Year's luncheon. Although the entertainment was almost entirely Japanese dancing and singing, a U.S. flag was posted on the stage and the event was opened by the Pledge of Allegiance led by a member of the Japanese American Citizens League. But following complaints by a few noncitizens, the next year the flag and pledge were missing.

In early 2005, the twenty-year-old saga of the Lawrence Street property that didn't sell took a new turn. The owner of the property on both sides of the association's parking lot offered to buy it for $468,750. It didn't take the association long to agree to sell the property that already had brought some $100,000 into the treasury.

chapter   ten

DECEMBER 7

On the night of Friday, December 5, 1941, a handful of Denver-
area Nisei met at the Japanese Association Hall to hear Utah-born
Mike Masaru Masaoka. Only weeks earlier he had been hired by the
national Japanese American Citizens League (JACL) in San Francisco as its executive secretary.

Masaoka was on a recruiting mission. He was seeking support
for the young and inexperienced organization of West Coast Nisei
whose leadership was deeply concerned about what would happen to
Japanese Americans if war should break out between the land of their
birth, citizenship, and loyalty and the land of their ancestry. On the
West Coast there was growing alarm as Washington and Tokyo appeared to be on a collision course because of American anger over
Japanese aggression in China. Masaoka, in his autobiography *They
Call Me Moses Masaoka,* wrote of his stop in Denver: "Right after

Thanksgiving I packed a suitcase and took the train for Salt Lake City en route to Denver, Greeley, Cheyenne, and points East. The reaction I encountered among Nisei in those towns was widely mixed. In some areas there was virtually no real awareness even among Nisei of worsening U.S.-Japan relations, little concern about what might happen to Japanese Americans in case of war. That was understandable. The integration of Nisei in many inland communities was well advanced, and many felt no need for JACL, which of course had been my position in Salt Lake City some years earlier. In Denver's small Nisei group, I found it difficult to stir up much interest in JACL."

In another chapter of his book Masaoka wrote, "I spoke about the Japanese American Citizens League's efforts to make the public aware that we were Americans, and about our need to win the recognition and backing of officials at all levels of government. On a map tacked to a wall, I pointed out the location of JACL chapters already in existence in inland areas and the places where I hoped new chapters would be formed, drawing circles of emphasis around places like Cheyenne, Denver, Pueblo, Scottsbluff, and North Platte. Inadvertently I was also outlining potential military targets—Cheyenne and Denver were the sites of air bases, Pueblo had a strategic steel mill, and North Platte was a railroad center."

On Saturday, December 6, Masaoka boarded a train for North Platte. The next day, December 7, Masaoka was addressing some fifty or sixty Japanese Americans—probably the largest gathering of Nisei in the history of the area—who had been assembled by Kano, the Christian minister. Masaoka was in the middle of his presentation when two federal officials, who did not identify themselves, broke up the meeting and took Masaoka to the local jail. Only later did he learn that, without warning, Japanese navy planes had bombed the Pearl Harbor U.S. naval base in Hawaii with heavy loss of ships and life.

On the West Coast, the impact on Japanese American communities of this act of war was almost instantaneous. Federal authorities accompanied by local officers quickly appeared at the homes of hundreds of Issei community leaders and took them away. The Nisei—U.S. citizens—were not detained but fear, confusion, and anger were widespread. The hostility toward Japanese that had lain dormant for decades until Japan invaded China surfaced in angry and alarmist press treatment. In Colorado the Japanese were largely spared the West Coast's harassment. But Nisei and their alien parents watched anxiously as the cry for "getting rid of the Japs" grew in California.

On February 19, 1942, President Franklin D. Roosevelt signed Executive Order 9066 authorizing the Army to designate certain "military areas" from which "any or all persons" could be excluded. General John L. DeWitt established a prohibited zone that included the western half of California (later extended to include the entire state), the southern half of Arizona, the western halves of Oregon and Washington, and all of Alaska. And "any or all persons" effectively meant "all persons of Japanese ancestry," "both alien and non-alien"—and never mind the legal rights of U.S. citizens. This development was almost as distressing to Japanese Americans in Colorado as to those in the designated areas, but they were relieved for the time being that Colorado was not designated as an exclusion area. Ten days later, on February 29, 1942, Colorado's Republican governor Ralph L. Carr issued a statement that Colorado would be willing to provide temporary shelter for law-abiding Japanese, Germans, and Italians ordered removed from the West Coast. He declared, "They are as loyal to American institutions as you and I. Many of them have been born here and are American citizens with no connection with or feeling of loyalty toward the customs and philosophies of Italy, Germany and Japan."

Under Executive Order 9066, signed by President Roosevelt on February 19, 1942, all persons of Japanese ancestry, "alien and non-alien," on the West Coast were herded into concentration camps, one of which was in Colorado.

The West Coast press, far from defending the rights of Japanese Americans, demanded their outster.

Women and children, the lame and the ill and the blind, were forced to leave their homes and enter prison camps.

In the face of widespread hostility toward Japanese Americans, Carr made his position even clearer on several occasions. On April 7, 1942, the newly organized federal War Relocation Authority (WRA), headed by Dr. Milton Eisenhower, summoned governors from fourteen Western states to Salt Lake City to ask their cooperation in resettling Japanese Americans displaced from coastal states. Carr was the only governor to support Eisenhower, declaring the Japanese Americans had every right to live in his state and Colorado would welcome them. By contrast, according to historian Mike Mackey, Wyoming governor Nels Smith shook his fist at Eisenhower and roared, "If you bring Japanese into my state, I promise they will be hanging from every tree."

Aerial view of the Amache relocation camp near Granada, Colorado, where more than 7,000 Japanese Americans were imprisoned during World War II.

All this rhetoric concerned the federal government's removal of Japanese Americans from prohibited zones, thereby making them displaced persons forced to fend for themselves in inland areas. It soon became obvious that public hostility made such a policy not only impractical but dangerous. The solution was to build ten huge, primitive "relocation centers"—a euphemism for concentration camps—to warehouse the ethnic Japanese in sparsely populated areas of the interior. WRA chose to place relocation camps in remote locations such as northwestern Wyoming, midway between Cody and Powell, and near the town of Granada in southeastern Colorado not far from the Kansas border. Only a handful of Japanese—perhaps a thousand—moved to Colorado before the Army halted "voluntary

Signs like this sprouted in West Coast states as Japanese American families, as potential "security risks," prepared for expulsion.

evacuation" on March 19, 1942, with an order making it illegal for Japanese Americans to either stay in their homes or leave them.

Carr was bitterly criticized in his state but he continued to defend his position vigorously even though he was in the middle of a hot election contest with popular Democrat Edwin (Big Ed) Johnson for the U.S. Senate. Johnson declared that Carr should use the National Guard to "close the borders to wandering Japanese migrants, whether citizens of the United States or not." Carr, although widely criticized as a "Jap lover," did not hesitate to continue standing up for the rights of Japanese Americans. He lost the Senate election by 3,642 votes out of a total of 375,000 cast. Political observers said Carr would easily have been elected to the Senate had he remained silent on the Japanese American issue.

What was the reason for Carr taking the position that he did? Certainly there were not enough votes in the Japanese American community—only a few hundred at most—to make it politically worth-

The evacuees were housed in flimsy barracks. Here men stuff straw into makeshift mattresses.

Meals in the camps, prepared by the evacuees themselves and served cafeteria style, were monotonous and meager at best.

while to defy widespread hostility and woo their support. Were there individual Japanese Americans who had access to Carr to plead for his support?

This matter was addressed by Dr. Joseph Norio Uemura, then the Hanna Professor of Philosophy at Hamline University in St. Paul, Minnesota, in a letter to the author dated February 6, 1996. He wrote,

> I hope it is not untoward, now, after over fifty years, to suggest that my father, the Rev. Seijiro Uemura, who was pastor of the Japanese Methodist Episcopal Church in Denver from 1929–1947, was highly instrumental in leading Governor Carr and Attorney General [Charles C.] Morrisey to their decision. Had my father and the church community [now the Simpson church] not been on excellent terms with these political figures, I trust

you will understand that Carr's invitation would never have happened.

Of course, one also must not forget the names of my father's colleagues, Samuel Marble of Trinity Church, Edgar Wahlbert of Grace Church, Harold Gilmore of the Colorado Council of Churches, the Denver Ministerial Alliance, and many others in the Christian community. It seems to me that the Japanese community in Denver has never even been aware of such an influence, let alone ever properly credited those very important people in the history of the Japanese Americans in Denver. And just once, it would be nice to acknowledge such in print.

The details of how the deeply respected Uemura influenced Carr's decision would be fascinating to know. But it may be that the seeds of understanding were planted long before Carr began public life. There are some who recall Carr, who died in 1950, as the quintessential lower case democrat whose beliefs about democracy and fairness developed early in his career as a small town attorney in poverty-stricken parts of Colorado, particularly in Antonito, a heavily Hispanic area in the southwest corner of the state. But it does not seem likely he was aware to any extent of the Japanese in Colorado before the outbreak of war. Eiichi Imada wrote in his newspaper in 1980:

[T]he increasingly strained relationship between Japan and America prompted the Japanese American Citizens League to hold a meeting at the Metropolitan Hotel in Denver in October, 1941. Gov. Ralph Carr was invited as the main speaker. He said that although he had been invited to many meetings by different races in this country of immigrants, he did not know much about the Japanese people. Having heard this speech, the then president of the Japanese Association, Dr. Konai Miyamoto, went to visit Governor Carr and explain the history of Japan and the history of Japanese immigrants in Colorado. He also told Carr about the contributions of the labor contractors who sent Japanese immigrants to farms and various construction sites in Colorado. This helped the governor to have a better understanding of the Japanese.

The Japanese Association, in an account published on the occasion of its eighty-fifth anniversary banquet in 1992, declared that "according to one report" Carr was influenced by "some Issei leaders." The source of this report is not identified, but the program says, "[S]hortly after the outbreak of war some Issei leaders, including Dr. Konai Miyamoto, called on Carr to discuss the possibility of harm coming to Japanese residents. Carr admitted that he knew very little about the Japanese in Colorado. His visitors then related the history of Japanese contributions to the state and their loyalty and dedication to their adopted home, and he promised he would do everything possible to protect them."

What casts a shadow over this account is that Issei, including the venerable Dr. Miyamoto, spoke very limited English and the effectiveness of their access to the statehouse can be questioned because they had no vote. This was decades before the appearance in postwar public life of a new generation of Japanese Americans like Stanley Matsunaka, president of the Colorado state senate; Dr. Melvin Takaki, mayor of Pueblo, the state's third largest city at the time; state senator Seiji Horiuchi, who impressed members of the Colorado legislature so much that he was talked of as a possible candidate for governor before he quit politics to go into private business. Of Nisei like Bob Sakata, a powerhouse in state and national agricultural circles, and civic leaders Jim Kanemoto of Longmont, Kiyoshi Otsuka in far northeast Colorado, Roy Inouye in the San Luis Valley in the opposite corner of the state, and the Wyenos of the Arkansas Valley. They, alas, were too young or had yet to be born.

It also has been suggested, perhaps cynically, that Carr was influenced by awareness of the need for laborers in the sugar beet and potato fields to replace the state's young men being called into service. His dedication to fair play and democracy, however, has never been challenged. Of Scotch-Irish stock, Carr was born in 1887 and spent much of his youth in the Cripple Creek mining area. William Wei, professor of history at the University of Colorado, has written,

> He [Carr] credited his experiences in the [mining] camps with giving him a compassion for those who, like Carr himself, came from modest circumstances. To Lee Casey of the *Rocky Mountain News* Carr expressed the hope that as a two-term governor he had not lost touch with my roots "because when I do, I shall cease to be the human being I've always been since those peculiar but interesting days in that great Colorado mining camp. My life has been spent in close contacts with people. I love people."

On another occasion Carr declared to a group of Coloradans threatening the Japanese arriving under military guard at the Granada camp in late August 1942: "If you harm them, you must first harm me. I was brought up in small towns where I knew the shame and dishonor of race hatred. I grew up to despise it because it threatened the happiness of you, and you and you." And addressing a labor union gathering, he said, "I am not in sympathy with those who demand that all evacuees be placed in concentration camps, regardless of their American citizenship or of the legality of their presence here. Our Constitution guarantees to every man, before he is deprived of his freedom, that there be charges and proof of misconduct in a fair hearing."

After his defeat Carr went back to his law practice, specializing in water issues, until he was persuaded to run for governor in 1950. He died unexpectedly during the campaign. But he was far from forgotten, although it took some time for his courage and wisdom to be honored. In 1976 the Japanese American community placed a bust of the governor in Sakura Square in downtown Denver. The inscription reads:

> In the hysteria of World War II, when others in authority forgot the noble principles that make the United States unique, Colorado's Governor Ralph L. Carr had the wisdom and courage to speak out on behalf of the persecuted Japanese American minority. "They are loyal Americans," he said, "sharing only race with the enemy." He welcomed them to Colorado to take part in the state's war effort and such were the times that this forthright act may have doomed his political future. Thousands came, seeking refuge from the West Coast's hostility, made new homes and remained to contribute much to Colorado's civic, cultural and economic life. Those who benefited from Governor Carr's humanity have built this monument in grateful memory of his unflinching Americanism and as a lasting reminder that the precious democratic ideals he espoused must forever be defended against prejudice and neglect.

Carr may be the only Colorado governor memorialized in three locations. In 1974 the Japanese Association placed a plaque honoring Carr on one of the columns outside the governor's office in the capitol. Former governor Dick Lamm once said that when he faced difficult political decisions he would walk out into the lobby and study the plaque. Then, inspired by the memory of his predecessor's courage to do what was right despite the consequences, Lamm would return to his office to make a decision.

The third memorial, on the southeast corner of the capitol grounds, was sponsored by the Colorado Bar Association and a committee headed by John Castellano, a former state legislator. On the day of the dedication then governor Roy Romer was in southern Utah to witness President Clinton sign a document establishing a vast new national monument. But he left a letter to be read at the dedication:

> I am very sorry that I am not able to be with you today. I have a personal interest in this memorial because Ralph Carr has always been one of my heroes. I lived within 12 miles of Camp Amache and I visited it on many occasions. In fact, I even went to the compound to play high school football with the kids who lived in the camp.
>
> These kids were American kids just like we were. For this reason, I always believed it was wrong to do what we did with Japanese Americans during the war. I could not understand how American citizens could be treated that way. But Ralph Carr was the only leader in the United States who had the courage to speak out openly against the way Japanese Americans were being treated. Given the times and the feelings of the times, that was a courageous act. Although he knew it might cost him his political career, he stood up when no one else would and did what was right.
>
> This is why he is a personal hero of mine, and that is why I am glad we honor him today. I thank all of you who have made this memorial possible—your hard work and your dedication to reminding us of our state's heritage and history are invaluable.

In 1996 the Colorado legislature passed a resolution honoring Carr for his "efforts to protect Americans of Japanese descent during World War II." And the *Denver Post,* which had been one of Carr's most strident critics in 1942, selected Carr as Colorado's "Person of the Century" for his humane leadership during one of the nation's most troubled times.

GRANADA

Within a month after Executive Order 9066 empowered the Army to remove Japanese Americans from designated areas, the federal government established the War Relocation Authority (WRA) to deal with the problem of what to do with the displaced people.

As mentioned in Chapter 10, Western governors summoned to a meeting in Salt Lake City had made it clear that simply scattering the evacuees throughout the interior was not only impractical but inviting disaster and even bloodshed. The "relocation centers" established by the WRA provided shelter for the inmates and, not so incidentally, kept the Japanese American inmates under military control.

Certain criteria had to be observed in selecting sites large enough to accommodate thousands of persons and keep them under guard. Preferably, the land should be government-owned and isolated from population centers. The sites had to have water and power. They also needed railroad access to bring in food and other supplies, many scores of barracks to house the inmates, a hospital, fire station, and schools.

Ten sites were selected, four of them in deserts: Manzanar in the Owens Valley of inland southern California whose water had been diverted to Los Angeles decades earlier; Poston and Gila River on desolate Indian reservations in southern Arizona; Topaz in the Sevier Desert of Utah. The other six were Tule Lake on the bed of a drained lake in northern California close to the Oregon border; Minidoka in Idaho's Snake River Valley; Heart Mountain on a partially completed irrigation project in north-central Wyoming; Rowher and Jerome in the Mississippi bottomlands of Arkansas; and Granada (also known as Amache) in the Arkansas River Valley of flat and windswept southeastern Colorado at the western edge of the Dust Bowl.

For Granada, the War Relocation Authority purchased several privately owned but undeveloped parcels of land near the town of that name to create a 10,500-acre preserve that straddled U.S. Highway 50. Work on the campsite—fencing in the site and building a town from scratch—began June 12, 1942, with as many as one thousand workmen employed at one time. By the end of August the evacuees, mostly from the Santa Anita and Merced temporary assembly centers in California, began to arrive by the trainload with only the ill having the luxury of sleeping berths on the four- or five-day trip. The last leg of the weary journey to Granada was not encouraging; on both sides of the tracks the view was only flat, sage-pocked grazing land stretching to the distant horizon.

There is much to support the contention that Granada was the most "peaceful" of the ten camps, however, because Granada's inmates expressed less unrest and resentment than in other camps about being imprisoned, unpalatable food, heat, cold, dust, and boredom. One reason may have been the close proximity of the town of Granada,

With no one to take over the businesses they were forced to abandon, Japanese American merchants held desperation sales.

in easy walking distance from the camp entry gate. Although there was little to attract internees to the town, morale was boosted by the ability—after camp life had settled into a routine—to get a pass at the gate and walk to Granada to enjoy the freedom of strolling through stores and buying soft drinks or snacks not served in a mess hall. These freedoms might have contributed to 99.8 percent of those in Amache (the highest percentage of all camps) answering affirmatively to No. 28—the loyalty question—on the government's ill-advised loyalty test questionnaire. One attraction in the later stages of the camp's life was a fresh fish market in the town of Granada established by ex-inmate Frank Tsuchiya, a veteran of the fish business in Los Angeles. Because he could not operate a private business in the camp, Tsuchiya after getting his release opened a store in the town where he sold *sashimi* fish shipped in by his prewar California suppliers. Prisoners from the camp allowed to visit the town would pick up a supply for themselves and friends and enjoy the delicacy in their barracks rooms with rice from the mess halls.

Generally the townspeople were friendly, or at least not unfriendly. This probably was partially the result of their familiarity with Japanese families who had been valley residents for decades and had proven to be good neighbors. And perhaps partly because the evacuees had responded to calls for help from area farmers at harvest time. And, of course, partly because they had money to spend.

The camp's own extensive agricultural program, giving the inmates a sense of accomplishment, also may have been a factor in the relative absence of internal unrest. A federal Department of Agriculture report published in 1999 said, "In spite of its small population*

_____

*At its peak the camp population was 7,318, in contrast with 18,789 at Tule Lake and 17,814 at Poston.

Granada had one of the largest and most diversified agricultural enterprises of the ten relocation centers. The farm program included
the raising of vegetable crops, feed crops, beef and dairy cattle, poul-
try, and hogs. Even the camp high school had a 500-acre farm operated by vocational agriculture students. Granada had an advantage
over other centers in that its fields and canals were already in place,
needing only minor repairs. Existing agricultural facilities were in-
corporated into the center's farm program: for example the relocation center's dairy made use of an existing dairy farm."

The schooling of camp children was a major concern. Modupe
Labode, chief historian of the Colorado Historical Society, has written in the Society's newsletter:

> The Granada Center's schools opened in October 1942 with over
> 530 high school students. There were so many children that
> students attended schools in shifts and improvised classrooms in
> the barracks were overcrowded. The WRA recruited white
> teachers to teach in the schools. Some of the teachers were
> dedicated and committed to providing the best possible experi-
> ence for the students. Others, stunned by the conditions at the
> relocation center, left after a short time. . . .
>
> The director of the Granada Relocation Center, James
> Lindley, recognized that classrooms and libraries in barracks were
> not satisfactory. He obtained approval from the federal govern-
> ment to construct a high school and elementary school. Once
> plans for the high school became public, Colorado newspapers
> and politicians pounded on the issue and played to anti-Japanese
> hysteria. The *Denver Post* and other newspapers ran articles
> claiming that the proposed schools were a waste of money and
> were "coddling" people who sympathized with the enemy.
> Senator Edwin Johnson exploited this bigotry and argued that
> the proposed high school was "extravagant and out of proportion."

Labode writes that the principal of Amache High was "determined that this school should be like other high schools throughout the country. . . . The WRA defined the 'primary task' of Amache High as encouraging the 'understanding of American ideals and loyalty to American institutions and to train students for the responsibilities of citizenship.'" Extolling the virtues of American democracy to citizens imprisoned for no reason other than their race was not an easy assignment.

The routine—and boredom—of camp life was shattered one day in October 1943 by an incident that might have had comic opera overtones if it weren't for its seriousness. Three Nisei sisters of the Shitara family, all married and in their thirties, were arrested on charges of having helped two German prisoners of war to escape. The women were Tsuruko (Toots) Wallace, age thirty-four; Florence (Flo) Shizue Otani, age thirty-three; and Billie Tanigoshi, age thirty-one. They were graduates of a high school in the Los Angeles suburb of Inglewood and had been shipped off to Granada.

Bored with life in the Granada camp, the three had responded to a call for volunteers to help with the harvest on area farms. They were assigned to Lloyd T. Winger's onion farm about twenty miles from Trinidad. Not far from Trinidad was a detention camp for German prisoners of war and Winger also had several of them assigned to his farm for work during the day, returning them to their camp at night. But for Japanese Americans released for farm work, there were virtually no restrictions. Winger provided them with a house, and they had a car and were free to do whatever they wished after the day's work. But town was a long distance away, and there wasn't much to do after work on the farm. Perhaps it was inevitable that Flo, Toots, and Billie should become friendly with Corporal Heinrich Haider and Corporal Herman Loescher, two Germans who had been captured in Africa. Sent to the Trinidad prison camp, they were among those released during the day for farm work.

Details of what happened were reported in court, but a brief outline of the events that led to the arrest and imprisonment of the three women is sufficient here. On the night of October 13, 1944, it was testified, the women left a package in the bushes near where the Germans had been working. The package, which the Germans picked up, contained men's civilian clothing, a flashlight, road maps, and some money.

After dark on October 17 the women drove to a road near the German POW camp six miles from Trinidad. Haider and Loescher had tunneled under the fence and were waiting behind a signboard. They entered the car and all five headed southward. Just past Wagon Mound, New Mexico, the men left the car and the women drove back to the farm. Two days later the Germans were picked up in a small village tavern by New Mexico highway patrolmen who had been alerted about the strangers in town. The Germans talked. Shortly, the women were arrested by FBI agents for helping the prisoners to escape. Bond was set at $10,000 each. Although the press had a field day, federal authorities said espionage was not involved and that the maps found on the Germans were gas station handouts with no military value.

Nearly a year later the three women were tried in a Denver federal court—with extensive and detailed coverage in the Denver press—and found guilty of conspiracy to commit treason. All three were sent to the federal correctional institution in Alderson, West Virginia. The two younger sisters were released after serving seventeen months of twenty-month sentences. Tsuruko Wallace, who had received a two-year term, also had her sentence reduced. By then the war was over. Reports of the time indicate the women's fellow inmates at the Granada camp were never sympathetic. Once they were assured that the sisters had not committed treason, the women were looked down upon for having let the temptation of romance overcome good sense.

When WRA established a new policy in 1943 encouraging detainees to "relocate" from the camps to freedom and normal lives in inland communities, it was natural that many in Granada would look to Denver. Before the war, Denver's Japanese population had been less than a thousand. During the period of "voluntary" evacuation, an estimated one thousand additional Japanese Americans moved to Denver and the farming areas north of the city.

During the period of resettlement in the latter stages of WRA life and after the camps were closed, Denver's Japanese population more than doubled again, and the appearance of the area around Twentieth and Larimer Streets, where their business enterprises congregated, changed abruptly. The square block between Larimer and Lawrence and Nineteenth and Twentieth was almost solidly Japanese. Newspapers of the time published ads for Yamamoto Barber Shop at 1836 Larimer, Clark Taketa Barber Shop at 1920 Larimer, Jack & Lloyd Nisei Barber Shop at 1957 Larimer, Kageyama Barber Shop at 1227 Twentieth Street, R. L. Young Insurance Agency at 604 Patterson Building, Drs. Y. and T. Ito, dentists, at 830 Eighteenth Street, Henry C. Takahashi's Pacific Watch Works at 1930 Lawrence, Attorney Taul Watanabe at 830 Eighteenth Street, Victory Cleaners at 1726 Larimer, Ohashi Beauty Salon on Eighteenth Street opposite the post office, Tea Pot Inn (Soldiers Welcome!) at 1814 Larimer, Ben's Grill at 2008 Larimer, T. K. Pharmacy at 2700 Larimer, and Lucky Florist at 1330 Twentieth Street.

Holding down one corner of Twentieth and Larimer was George Furuta's Manchu Chop Suey and Grill. It was never explained that authentic Manchurian cuisine does not include chop suey, but the

Manchu became a popular hangout and sometime nightclub with the expansive Furuta as master of ceremonies. Across the street on one side was the Mandarin restaurant that featured Japanese dishes. On the other was Fred's Pool where Fred Aoki's billiards hall was in back with his wife's Akebono Japanese restaurant (featuring grilled mackerel) in front. Elsewhere around the block were Nonaka's barbershop, George Fukuma's hardware store, Yutaka Akiyoshi's pool hall, an employment agency, a photographer, insurance agents, Mits Kaneko's accounting office, and the Pacific Market, which sold Japanese foodstuffs. On the Lawrence Street side were such enterprises as Nakayama's confectionary plant, George Kuramoto's gas station, and the Granada Fish Market, which Frank Tsuchiya had moved up from the town of Granada in partnership with Frank Torizawa. It is said that Torizawa had only $5 left in the cash register on opening day after paying all his start-up bills.

Denver's Granada Fish Market deserves special mention because, despite its humble beginnings, it helped to change the eating habits of an entire city. Until the outbreak of war, about the only fresh fish conveniently available at reasonable prices to supplement salt cod in the diet of landbound Denverites was farm-raised trout, catfish, and carp. After Tsuchiya returned to Los Angeles to resume wholesaling fresh fish, Torizawa's iced display cases featured a wide variety from both coasts—fresh salmon and tuna, crab and oysters, mackerel and perch, red snapper and swordfish—that drew customers from all parts of the city. The Sakura Square urban renewal project (to be discussed in a later chapter) forced the Granada to move to Larimer Street. Shortly after Torizawa sold the business to Japanese investors and retired, the fish market was closed.

Some transplants saw an opportunity in providing for the tastes of the Japanese population in other ways. Densuke Kanegae founded the Denver Sake Brewing Company, which had competition from Colorado Sake Brewery at 2845 Walnut Street. Other businesses producing Japanese foodstuffs included the Denver Noodle Factory, Nakamura's *miso* and soy sauce plant, and Kojima's Soybean Food Manufacturing Company whose main product was tofu.

As a Japanese American population center, Denver also became a site for a JACL service office. Joe Grant Masaoka, older brother of Mike, set up a small office downtown to help relocated Japanese from the camps find jobs and housing and to intercede in cases of harassment or discrimination. When Joe Masaoka returned to California in 1947 after the war, Roy Takeno took over as JACL representative until 1951 when he left for a more secure job in state government.

On Thursday nights the YWCA would sponsor dances for the Japanese Americans. Why Thursdays? Because Thursday was the maids' night off and many Nisei girls had taken jobs as maids and housekeepers to get out of the camps.

Other Japanese American enterprises started in Colorado during the war and early postwar era have not only survived but prospered. Four of them were among the fifty Japanese American businesses, operated by three generations of the same family, that were honored in early 2003 by the Japanese American National Museum of Los Angeles for having helped "Build the American Dream." Their citations, slightly abbreviated, follow:

LAFAYETTE FLORISTS OF LAFAYETTE: A brand new gift shop and garden center stands today where Yasutaro and Kumiko Yoshihara began their small fruit stand flower shop in 1949. Originally from California, the Yoshihara family started Lafayette Florist after being released from camp in Amache, Colorado. In 1960 their oldest son, Gene, and his wife, Evelyn, took over the business and built a new building for the flower shop. In the next decade the business became a major wholesale grower of Colorado carnations. With the change in the carnation market, the garden center division was created and the operation went from wholesale to retail. Daughters Lori Wheat and Sandi Yoshihara-Sniff and their husbands are all actively involved in the business. . . . Today, Lafayette Florist occupies 68,000 square feet of greenhouses and two floors of gift showrooms. Its commemorative poster states, "Dreams are reachable. They take shape in the children we raise, the seeds we sow, the gardens we tend, and the causes we champion."

PACIFIC MERCANTILE COMPANY, DENVER: George (Yutaka) Inai came to America in 1915 from Japan with the dream of owning his own business. Originally settling in Sacramento, California, the family spent the war years in camp at Topaz, Utah, and Tule Lake, California. Close family friends George and Wesley Oyama recommended the Denver area (for resettlement). They were to become George's first business partners in an Asian grocery store, which opened in 1944. . . . Pacific Mercantile Company served the Asian American community in Colorado, including the early Japanese farmers. George's children, Susan, Sam and Robert, continued to successfully run the family business and developed a culturally diverse customer base. George's grandchildren, Kyle, Jolie and Keith, along with their mother Susan, now operate the business, which has been called Denver's premier Asian grocery store. . . . In 2002 it was named one of the top six businesses in downtown Denver by the Downtown Denver Partnership.

TAGAWA GREENHOUSES, INC., BRIGHTON: From sharecropping in Colorado to operating more than 1,600,000 square feet of greenhouses in Colorado and California, the Tagawa family survived incarceration during World War II to become one of the largest plant growers in the United States. Frank Shigeo and Hazel Haruko Tagawa came from the Yuba City area of California and grew vegetables before being sent to camp at Amache, Colorado. After the war he worked as a sharecropper and truck farmer in Welby, Colorado, moving around with his wife and six children, Ken, Albert, Dave, George, Jim and Caroline. Eventually he bought 120 acres outside of Brighton and the family began by growing vegetables and seedlings in a few wooden-frame greenhouses. With their farming knowledge, they diversified by growing carnations, roses and spring bedding plants. In addition to the greenhouse business, they operate a garden center and florist in Parker. They are also active in the academic community with ongoing plant research and scholarships. Currently, there are four brothers, three wives, and ten nieces and nephews that work in the family business.

TWENTIETH STREET CAFE, DENVER: It took a few years for Harry Okuno and his wife Sugi to restart the restaurant business in Denver that they left behind in Hollywood, California, when the war broke out. After incarceration at Amache (Granada), the Okunos moved to Denver. Taking over the Twentieth Street Cafe, which retained the same name from its previous owners, the Okunos soon enlisted their son, Ted, to help. Ted and his wife, Ann, took over, and together they cooked and served customers breakfast, lunch, and dinner for more than fifty years. In 1972 their son, Rod, returned from running a ski shop in Park City, Utah, to begin working at the restaurant. When his parents retired two years ago, Rod and his wife, Carol, settled into a business that came naturally to them. . . . Using many of the same American recipes that his father and grandfather originated, Rod likes to feature an occasional Asian dish. Since Rod is presently the only cook, he is seen working long and hard hours in a business that relies heavily on customer satisfaction.

Today, Colorado has more than 10,000 residents of Japanese extraction, many of whom first came to the state to be confined behind the Granada camp's barbed wire fences. To honor those who lived through that sorry experience and to make sure that camp would not be forgotten, the Denver Central Optimists Club, founded in 1979 with a primarily Nisei membership, decided in 1981 to memorialize the site as a club project.

When a group of them went to inspect the campsite they found only desolation—the broken foundations of the barracks, dying remnants of the Russian olive and cottonwood trees the inmates had planted in search of shade, sagging barbed wire, and a town dump not far away. Most moving was the tiny cemetery where plaques laid flush with the ground were barely visible through the weeds. There were seven or eight that carried the names of infants who were stillborn or had died within a few days of birth.

At the edge of the cemetery was a small, sturdy brick vault that at one time had sheltered a Buddhist altar. In the vault was a wooden plaque with an epitaph in Japanese written with brush and ink, now fading. In translation, it read:

We set foot on this site, the Amache wartime relocation center, on August 27, 1942, from the Merced, California, assembly center and were to spend the next three full years as internees until our release. During this period, thirty-one young men from Amache laid down their lives on foreign soil in the defense of America, and in addition, over one hundred ten individuals succumbed while incarcerated here. Upon termination of the global conflict and the closing of this camp, all internees will be scattering to the four winds. In spite of the strong camaraderie we came to know over the long and trying years, and the many fond memories we hold so dear, it shall be ever so difficult to revisit these grounds. Moreover, we seven thousand plus Japanese who survived the long and painful ordeal as brothers and sisters will be leaving this site, but shall forever cherish the memory of our departed friends and relatives. Lest we forget, in final tribute, we who are departing these grounds forever hereby erect this small monument to their memory.

> September 6, 1945
> Granada, Colorado
> In the names of all internees
> during the war years

It was indeed a small monument, meaningful only to the few who knew of its existence. The Optimists made it their project to build a more permanent memorial. Over the Labor Day weekend in 1983 the Optimists led a pilgrimage of Denverites to the campsite to dedicate a granite monument. Today it stands tall above the prairie grass, bearing the names of the 31 Granada Nisei men—out of the 494 who left the camp to join the armed forces—who gave their lives for their country in World War II:

John Akimoto	Victor Akimoto	Kunio Hattori
Chikara Inouye	Frank T. Kanda	Saburo Kuratsu
Haruo Kawamoto	Leo Kikuchi	John Kimura
Mamoru Kinoshita	Eizo Masuda	Peter Masuoka
Haruto Moriguchi	Akira Morihara	Kiyoshi K. Muranaga
Masao Nakagaki	Ned Nakamura	Arnold Ohki
Katsunoshin Okida	Lloyd M. Onouye	Calvin Saito
George Saito	Masami Sakamoto	Masao Shigezane
Toshiaki Shoji	Robert S. Sueoka	Shigeo Tabuchi
Tadashi Takeuchi	Harry Tokushima	Bill Iwao Yamaji
Joe R. Yasuda		

Another face of the memorial carries this message under the heading "Amache Remembered":

Dedicated to the 31 patriot Japanese Americans who volunteered from Amache and dutifully gave their lives in World War II, to

the approximately 7,000 persons who were relocated at Amache
and to the 120 who died here during this period of relocation.
August 27, 1942, October 15, 1945.

It was on that date that the last eighty-five involuntary residents left,
and Colorado's prison camp became no more.

Every Memorial Day members of the club, friends, and a dwindling number of Amache survivors drive to the campsite for a service
of remembrance. Over the years, the Optimists, together with students from Granada High School led by their teacher John Hopper,
have beautified the site. A Granada Preservation Society collects camp
artifacts, sponsors a research museum, and takes the Amache story
wherever there is interest. There is now a fence around the cemetery
area to keep out the cows. Donated sod and evergreen trees have
been planted. Pipe was laid by the students and their leaders to bring
water from a distant source to the plantings. When the Optimists
Club disbanded in 2005 because of dwindling membership, some
members formed the Amache Club to carry on the work of preserv-
ing the campsite.

On U.S. Highway 50, a short distance from the cemetery, are
signs identifying the place where a sad chapter of history was played
out.

chapter   twelve

THE ALIEN
LAND LAW

The growth of the Japanese American population in Denver
during the war years went relatively unnoticed, but that was not the
case in some rural areas of Colorado, particularly in Adams County
just north of Denver. Some residents began to view with alarm the
growing number of Japanese who were settling in the county and
sharecropping, leasing farms, or—horrors—buying land.

In January 1944 Colorado governor John Vivian received a delegation of Adams County farmers and businessmen headed by Mayor
J. W. Wells of Brighton. Wells declared that in the previous six months
an "alarming" number of Japanese had been buying farmland and
businesses in Adams County, often paying much more than the
property was worth. He said residents were fearful of "agricultural and business exploitation by the Japs" who previously had
been only renters or sharecroppers. If Wells explained where these

refugees from the West Coast were getting all that money, there is no record.

. The visitors proposed that, because the problem was so urgent, a special legislative session be called to pass an anti-alien land law, prohibiting ownership of real property by aliens ineligible to citizenship. Such a law existed in a number of states, primarily in the West. And because Japanese immigrants, like other Asians, were not permitted naturalization, the intent of such a law was only too evident.

In 1889 the state of Washington had been the first state to pass legislation prohibiting land ownership by aliens ineligible to citizenship. California had enacted a similar law in 1913 under the slogan "Keep California White" at a time when Japanese owned approximately 12,700 acres in the state out of a total of 11 million acres of improved farmland. Despite relatively few Asians living in most of these states, similar laws had been passed over the years by Oregon, Idaho, Nebraska, Texas, Kansas, Louisiana, Montana, New Mexico, Minnesota, and Missouri with the comprehensive California law serving as the pattern. Governor Vivian's aides pointed out to him that Article 2, Section 27, of Colorado's constitution recognized property rights of aliens with these words: "Aliens, who are or may hereafter become bona fide residents of this state, may acquire, inherit, possess, enjoy and dispose of property, real and personal, as native born citizens." Section 27 said nothing about requiring citizenship for land ownership, nor did it define "bona fide resident." It could be argued that there was no reason an alien ineligible to citizenship could not be a "bona fide" resident entitled to the right to own property.

Thus, Vivian was advised, the state constitution had no provision preventing Japanese Americans or even Japanese aliens from owning real property. Vivian then said he wasn't about to call a special legislative session to change the constitution but promised to look into the problem.

Meanwhile, the Brighton Chamber of Commerce passed a resolution saying the influx of aliens posed "a menace to the public welfare of citizens" and urged new legislation prohibiting land ownership by all aliens. Others seized on this idea. Attorney general Gail Ireland backed a proposal to call a special session of the legislature to pass a constitutional amendment that would have the effect of giving aliens a year to dispose of their property, with the state having the power to seize property after that deadline. In his opinion, the attorney general said, such an amendment would not violate either the national or state constitution.

A Constitutional Amendment Committee was established by the House and hearings were opened on February 7, 1944. Mayor Wells was the principal witness in favor of the proposed measure, but remarkably a number of citizens turned out to oppose the amendment. Among them were Dean Paul Roberts, the highly respected pastor of St. John's Episcopal Cathedral; Rev. John A Foote, who had been a missionary to Japan; Charles Binna, secretary of the Denver Congress of Industrial Organizations labor union; attorney Arthur Henry, a former legislator; attorney W. W. Grant; and Rev. Joseph Johnson Jr., president of the Colored Ministers Alliance. State representative Earl Mann, the sole black in the legislature, pled for defeat of the proposal on "behalf of 10,000 Negro soldiers from Colorado." The gist of the arguments against the proposed law was that it was racially discriminatory. The upshot was a decision to take the issue to the voters. An election on a constitutional amendment—to deny ownership of real property to aliens ineligible for citizenship, or to put it bluntly, the Japanese—was scheduled for October 29, 1944.

As election day neared, both sides stepped up efforts to gain public support. Mayor Wells's group brought in John R. Lechner, a longtime rabble-rousing foe of Japanese Americans who had been a loud advocate of the removal of Nisei from California in 1942. He had set himself up as president of an organization he called Americanism Education League of Los Angeles.

When Lechner, who claimed the title of Doctor, appeared at a mass meeting in Brighton a few days before the election to speak for the amendment, he was surprised to see in the audience Joe Grant Masaoka, representative of the Japanese American Citizens League in Denver. Masaoka asked to be heard and was given the stage where he forcefully but politely expressed his opposition to the amendment. When Masaoka showed up again the next night at another Lechner appearance, he was denied entry. At the third meeting Masaoka's entry was blocked by police. Mayor Wells's explanation was that Lechner had not been invited to Colorado to debate the amendment issue but merely to speak. Lechner argued that Japanese aliens cannot be assimilated into the American way of life and made the preposterous charge that Japanese farmers could undersell American farmers because of subsidies from Japan.

The proposed Anti-Alien Land Law amendment was defeated 184,458 to 168,865. Significantly, despite efforts by backers of the measure to whip up support by citing reports of atrocities by Japanese troops in the war then raging, a substantial number of absentee ballots cast by Coloradans in military service opposed the discriminatory measure.

There are some strange sidebars to this bit of history. Long after the episode was ended, Bob Sakata, whose remarkable success as farmer and citizen is told in another chapter of this book, learned that Wells had delivered the baby Joanna Tokunaga who was to become his wife. And on the death of the three men most closely associated with Wells's campaign—farmers George Mancini, Elbert Hattendorf, and Tom Litterell—their families asked Sakata to serve as pallbearer. He did. As for Brighton and Adams County, the Issei farmers and the Nisei who succeeded them have made vast contributions that have added immeasurably to the area's prosperity and progress. The annual chow mein dinner at the Adams County fairgrounds—sponsored by the Japanese American Association of Brighton to raise funds for scholarships and many other good community causes—is an informal social event supported by hundreds of their friends and neighbors.

After the war, a number of legal actions pertaining to the rights of Japanese aliens and citizenship took place nationally. In 1952 Congress passed the Walter-McCarran Act, which stated that "the right of a person to become a naturalized citizen of the United States shall not be denied or abridged because of race or sex." This opened the way for Issei, after decades as resident aliens, to attend civics classes and apply for citizenship. Soon the Japanese American Citizens League became involved in several legal challenges to the constitutionality of anti-alien land laws in California. One of the cases was filed by the six Masaoka brothers, five of whom—including Mike—had served in the military. They proposed to buy a home for their mother, Haruye, an alien who under the law could not own property. The Masaokas went to court. This time the judge, Thurmond Clarke of the Superior Court of Los Angeles, ruled the Alien Land Law unconstitutional because it was directed against persons of Japanese ancestry solely because of their race and Haruye was permitted to receive title to the house. In 1956 2.5 million California voters repealed the Alien Land Law by a two to one margin.

A noteworthy and often overlooked exception to hostility toward Japanese land ownership took place in Colorado's San Luis Valley where their presence was not only tolerated but solicited. In the early 1900s several land companies engaged in a vigorous competition to develop farming in the isolated valley. The largest was the Costilla Estates Company, which owned nearly 550,000 acres of undeveloped land, about a fifth of which was suitable for agriculture. By 1914 the property had been taken over by several developers, the leading one being the Gibson Land Company of Boston and Denver. It experienced only mediocre success until 1924 when, according to historian Dr. Morris C. Cohen, Roy Shahan of the Gibson Land Company and C. B. West and Richard Blakey of the Blakey and West Real Estate Company went to California to seek out Japanese farmers who might consider moving to the San Luis Valley. In Stockton they met with Yoshie Inouye, chairman of the local Japanese Association, and a Mr. K. Ono. Soon afterward, the two men visited the valley. Dr. Cohen has written:

> During the meetings with Japanese in Stockton, Mr. Inouye had introduced Mr. Shahan to a number of Association members. Among these [was] Mr. Eiichi Yoshida. In February of 1945 Mr. Yoshida brought his family by train to the San Luis Valley. He made no prior trip and brought very little with him, as he had been told that all he required would be provided by Mr. Shahan. The Yoshida family settled on a small farm in the Carmel district southwest of Alamosa, where they share-cropped a few acres belonging to the Gibson Co. Within a few weeks the Yojiro Hattori family arrived, followed by the Mori family, and in March the Toyosuke Ogura family settled in a two-room farmhouse near La Jara. None of these first families had made previous ventures to the Valley, and all share-cropped on farms owned by Gibson Co.
>
> Jintaro Katsumoto visited the San Luis Valley during the winter of 1924. . . . He found opportunities much to his liking, and in December 1925 he moved into the Valley where he

purchased a 60-acre farm five miles south of Alamosa on the Henry Road. This was the first purchased by a Japanese in the San Luis Valley. . . .

It was not until the spring of 1926 that Mr. Ono and Mr. Inouye came to the Valley. Mr. Ono purchased 80 acres of land at $125 per acre. . . . The first crop he produced consisted entirely of potatoes. Mr. Inouye arrived in April 1926 and rented 160 acres of land near La Jara from Mr. Blakey. . . .

It is extremely difficult to place the exact number of families coming to the San Luis Valley as a direct result of the Stockton meetings. Census figures for 1930 show a total of 233 Japanese living in the five counties comprising the Valley. . . .

The first arrivals faced many hardships including the long journey from California. The Ogura family was one of several to make the trip by automobile. The car was a 1923 Chevrolet open top and possessions were loaded on the running boards. The children got out of the car when steep upgrades were encountered and followed along behind. . . . During the two weeks required to make the trip, evenings were spent along the highways in auto camps. Mr. Ogura left California with only $100 in his pocket.

It is evident that Mr. Shahan, the land agent, kept his word about providing for the needs of the early arrivals. A number of Japanese recall that credit was advanced them by almost every business in Alamosa. This transpired at a time when credit was not easy to obtain. According to a few reports, the use of Mr. Shahan's name was enough to arrange purchase at many local stores. Mr. Shahan once arranged to have Japanese youngsters living several miles from Alamosa bussed into town in order that they might enjoy the benefits of larger schools. . . .

In 1923, prior to the arrival of the Japanese, only some 600 acres were producing a wide variety of vegetables. By 1925 over 4,000 acres were producing a wide variety of vegetables, and there were 11 packing houses in the south end of the valley. The increase is largely attributed to the Japanese. Perhaps the greatest attribute of early Japanese . . . was their honesty.

Columnist Virginia Simmons wrote in Alamosa's *Valley Courier* in 2002, "The Valley's Japanese Americans, past and present, have made significant contributions in several walks of life here, their family names being among our most admired. If we could turn back the clock, I think that most people would want to undo mistakes that were made under the influence of emotion, fear and prejudice."

To recognize the contributions of Japanese Americans in the valley, Adams State College in Alamosa has established a depository for papers and memorabilia about the Japanese Americans, and as this was written funds were being raised to build a Japanese memorial garden on the campus.

Long before the Japanese became a major factor in the San Luis Valley economy, a Denver Issei named Arthur F. Takamine had gained enough prominence to become known as the "Potato King." He marketed potatoes and onions through his company American Potato Company, located in Denver's Denargo Market. Its motto was "It Is Not a Meal Without Potato."

An advertisement Takamine published carried the following message:

> In season we handle Calif. White Rose, Bliss Triumph, also Bliss and Pontiac from Florida, Alabama, La., Okla., Tex., Ariz., and New Mexico. Russet Burbanks grown in Idaho, Oregon, Washington, Colorado, Utah. Dry Onions, Western and Southern grown Globes, Babosas, seed potatoes, Early Ohio, Bliss Triumphs and Irish Cobblers. State Certified Blue Tags from Minnesota, North Dakota. We have direct connections, Eastern terminal markets. To Nisei growers we would be glad to assist

any marketing problems you may have. Personal contact directly
with Arthur F. Takamine or Richie N. Takamine on carlot at
LCL lots. Denver the Queen City of the Plains, the distribution
center of the entire Middlewest, Welcomes your shipment!!!

Principals in the firm, in addition to Arthur and Richie, were Tol and
Terrie Takamine. Like the S. Harada Farms of the Arkansas Valley,
American Potato is no longer in business.

chapter   thirteen
THE PRESS

Early Japanese immigrants knew almost no English, but most of them despite their humble origins were literate in Japanese thanks to compulsory grade school education at home. Thus it is understandable that Japanese-language newspapers were among their first enterprises.

Colorado's first Japanese language publication—or, more accurately, printing endeavor—was probably Naoichi Hokasono's 1908 pamphlet outlining a code of behavior for immigrants to avoid drawing unfavorable attention to themselves (see Chapter 4).

Eiichi Imada's research has found that Hokasono then began a small daily called *Denba Shimpo* ("*Denver News*") publishing mostly local news items. Imada has written, "Two years later a group of students from Japan attending Colorado schools founded *Kororado Shimbun* ("*Colorado Newspaper*"). Among the editors was Toichiro Ichikawa, brother of Fusae Ichikawa who was a member of the Lower

House of the Japanese Parliament and women's rights activist. Ichikawa urged his readers to fight efforts to pass an anti-alien land law in Colorado. Whether this did any good is doubtful because his readers spoke little English, could not vote, and wielded little influence, but Ichikawa's stories made the Japanese aware of the problem. After graduation from the University of Denver, Ichikawa returned to Japan and became a professor at the Tokyo Institute of Technology.

As was common among early U.S. newspapers of any language, both *Denba Shimpo* and *Kororado Shimbun* had a hard time surviving. They merged as the *Santo Jiji* with Hokasono's support but he pulled out in 1917, selling the paper to a well-to-do farmer, Kakutaro Nakagawa, who renamed it *Kakushu Jiji* ("*Colorado Times*"). Put in charge of the paper were Minejiro Nakasugi and a young immigrant named Sojiro Yoritomo who had served with the U.S. Army in Europe in World War I. But faced with a dwindling Japanese population the paper failed to prosper. In 1929 the *Colorado Times* was sold for $4,500 to Nakasugi and Ichiro (Fred) Kaihara who became editor and later its owner.

The following year a young Buddhist priest named Yoshitaka Tamai came to Denver (see Chapter 8). He and the head priest, Rev. Yoshinao Ouchi, founded a weekly publication they called *Rokki* ("*Rocky*") *Nippon,* which was devoted largely to morality lessons and advice about family relations rather than to news.

During this period Japanese language newspapers that were devoted to local community news and news from Japan (with modest English sections for the Nisei) were being published in Los Angeles, San Francisco, Sacramento, Portland, and Seattle. With the outbreak of war in 1941 all were shut down. Abruptly, the only Japanese language newspapers in the United States, outside of New York, were the *Utah Nippo* in Salt Lake City, which changed its name to *Utah Times; Kakushu Jiji* in Denver, which became *Colorado Times;* and *Rokki Nippon,* which was renamed *Rocky Shimpo* ("*Rocky News*") and converted from a Buddhist newsletter into a tri-weekly under the ownership of Shiro Toda. These newspapers found an avid readership among the West Coast Japanese who had been moved into the camps and were starved for news. The surviving papers, which were not openly censored (although no doubt closely watched), enjoyed an unprecedented circulation boom that leveled off at around 10,000 copies for the *Colorado Times* and 8,000 for the *Rocky Shimpo,* but these figures may be suspect. The *Rocky Shimpo* carried a box on page one of the English section that boasted it was the "Largest Circulated Nisei Vernacular in Continental U.S.A."

The only other "Japanese" newspaper in the West was *Pacific Citizen,* which before the war was a sporadically published all-English house organ of the Japanese American Citizens League. When Japanese Americans were forced out of the West Coast, *Pacific Citizen* of necessity was moved to Salt Lake City and converted almost overnight into a tabloid-size eight-page weekly printed in a commercial shop. The entire staff was made up of Larry Tajiri and his wife, Marion, who in view of JACL's difficult financial straits worked for a pittance. Tajiri considered editing *Pacific Citizen* a duty to Japanese Americans rather than a job. He was a thoroughly capable professional, erudite, and a facile writer politically aware and dedicated. He had started with the English sections of Japanese language newspapers in Los Angeles and San Francisco and at the time war broke out was working in the New York bureau of the *Asahi,* Japan's leading newspaper. When federal authorities closed the *Asahi* office, Tajiri drove back to San Francisco in the newspaper's car, which he had received in lieu of severance pay, and volunteered his services at JACL headquarters.

On the eve of the evacuation deadline he and his wife drove to Salt Lake City. There they helped set up a JACL office in the Beason Building downtown, located a printer, and set out to publish a weekly paper that would provide both news and editorial leadership for confused, discouraged, distraught Japanese Americans eager for information. The *Pacific Citizen* under the Tajiris was professional, hard-hitting, and readable. But it was a weekly that was distributed by mail and, in trying to cover the entire Japanese American world, its coverage in any given community was thin. Furthermore, its circulation was limited to 8,000 by the paper shortage.

Toda, *Rocky Shimpo*'s editor and publisher, was one of the few Colorado Japanese questioned by federal authorities and the only one in the region detained other than Rev. Hiram Kano. In later years Toda liked to recall that he was asked by the federal official questioning him why, if he were loyal to the United States as he claimed, he hadn't become a naturalized citizen. Of course the answer was that the law denied him that right.

With Toda imprisoned and most other Japanese reluctant to take over, the family had no choice but to put their teenage daughter, Tetsuko Mary, in charge.* Of course she knew nothing about editing and publishing a newspaper. She and her advisers persuaded Haruo Muranaka to run the Japanese language section and hired as English section editor a San Francisco Nisei named James Matsumoto Omura, who was to become the center of perhaps the stormiest episode in the history of the Japanese American press.

Omura, a native of Washington state, had aspired to be a newspaperman in his youth but experienced little success. At the outbreak

---

*She survived the ordeal and in time married a farmer named Harry Matsunaka. They had a son named Stanley who studied law, entered politics, and served as president of the Colorado state senate.

of war he was working in the floral business in San Francisco and using his earnings to publish his own little monthly magazine, *Current Life,* with a claimed circulation of 500. It was started in October 1940 and carried essays, short stories, and commentary—much of it critical of the Nisei establishment—written by aspiring young Nisei writers.

Omura had testified at the San Francisco hearings of the Tolan Committee, a congressional committee formed early in 1942 to investigate "problems of evacuation of enemy aliens and others from prohibited military zones." There he had made his position, which was somewhat different from that of previous Nisei witnesses, quite clear.

Before Omura testified, the primary witness for the Nisei, Mike Masaoka, national secretary of the Japanese American Citizens League, had presented a lengthy statement which said in part:

> With any policy of evacuation definitely arising from reasons of military necessity and national safety, we are in complete agreement. As Americans citizens, we cannot and should not take any other stand. But, also, as American citizens believing in the integrity of our citizenship, we feel that any evacuation enforced on grounds violating that integrity should be opposed. If in the judgment of military and Federal authorities, evacuation of Japanese residents from the West Coast is a primary step toward assuring the safety of this nation, we will have no hesitation in complying with the necessities implicit in that judgment. But if, on the other hand, such evacuation is primarily a measure whose surface urgency cloaks the desires of political or other pressure groups who want us to leave merely from motives of self-interest, we feel that we have every right to protest and to demand equitable judgment on our merits as American citizens.

Omura said in his statement, "I requested to be heard here due largely to the fact that I am strongly opposed to mass evacuation of

American-born Japanese." On this point he was in agreement with JACL's position. But where he parted from JACL's stand was his contention that JACL was wrong in agreeing to cooperate with the government in their own imprisonment. "It is my honest belief," he said, "that such an action would not solve the question of Nisei loyalty. . . . I am in some measure opposed to what some of the other representatives of the Japanese community have said here before this committee. . . . I specifically refer to the JACL. It is a matter of public record among the Japanese community that I have been consistently opposed to the Japanese American Citizens League. . . . I have felt that the leaders were leading the American-born Japanese along the wrong channels, and I have not minced words in saying so publicly."

Then, addressing the congressmen directly, Omura asked, "Has the Gestapo come to America? Have we not risen in righteous anger at Hitler's mistreatment of the Jews? Then is it not incongruous that citizen Americans of Japanese descent should be similarly mistreated and persecuted?" He finished by assuring the congressmen that humanitarian treatment of Japanese Americans "would not endanger the national security of this country nor jeopardize our war efforts."

Omura's words were recorded and ignored as, no doubt, the testimony of others was ignored. The decision to remove ethnic Japanese from the West had been made days before the Tolan Committee hearings began. For a brief period, however, the Army permitted them to move inland on their own. Omura and his wife left for Denver before the deadline and tried, without success, to continue publishing his magazine. Then he found employment with *Rocky Shimpo*. Despite his lack of experience, he ran a credible news section. He also wrote a signed freewheeling personal opinion column titled "Nisei America Know the Facts."

It is now necessary to leap forward to February 1943 when the War Relocation Authority, the agency responsible for the detention camps, decided to require all adult prisoners to respond to a questionnaire ostensibly to determine their futures. The questionnaires were titled "Application for Leave Clearance," which indicated WRA was seeking information that would lead to releasing the evacuees. Two of the questions related to military service. Question No. 27 was "Are you willing to serve in the armed forces of the United States on combat duty, wherever ordered?" And Question No. 28 was "Will you swear unqualified allegiance to the United States of America and faithfully defend the United States from any and all attack by foreign or domestic forces, and foreswear any form of allegiance or obedience to the Japanese Emperor, or any other foreign government, power, or organization?"

Although most answered No. 27 and No. 28 affirmatively without qualms, pitfalls and shortcomings were obvious to anyone who knew anything about Japanese Americans and their plight. Some men said of course they would be willing to serve in the armed forces— if their rights as citizens were restored and their families were allowed to go home. However, there was no such assurance in the questionnaire. Others asked if they would be assigned to the segregated—some called it Jim Crow—Japanese American 442nd Regimental Combat Team. Or would they be allowed to serve in any branch of the service like other Americans? Some Issei, the immigrant generation, argued that because the United States denied them the right to become citizens, to foreswear allegiance to Japan in Question No. 28 would leave them people without a country. Some Nisei asked how it was possible to foreswear an allegiance that had never existed, and further, wouldn't forswearing such allegiance be an admission that it did exist? And because the questionnaire didn't distinguish between sexes, some women wondered if they would be drafted.

Despite these misgivings the great majority of those in the camps accepted the questionnaires, clumsy and confusing as they were, for what they were purported to be—a fact-finding measure leading to restoration of their·rights. But a minority regarded them as a loyalty test that would lead to forced military service with no assurance that grievances would be addressed. In the various camps skeptics organized campaigns to answer the controversial questions negatively and resist the draft call by refusing to appear for their pre-induction physical examinations.

JACL, which strongly endorsed restoration of Nisei eligibility for military service so they could step forward in an unmistakable demonstration of loyalty, was alarmed by the dissent. JACL feared any appearance of disloyalty would damage efforts to regain rights for all Japanese Americans. Joe Grant Masaoka, who was running JACL's Denver office, joined with Minoru Yasui in a determined effort to change the minds of dissidents. The book *JACL in Quest of Justice,* has this to say:

> JACL had in fact made considerable efforts to help some of the
> draft resisters. Joe Grant Masaoka and Min Yasui first met with
> Nisei from the Amache camp at Granada being held at the
> Federal Correctional Institute outside Denver. Yasui, who had
> gone to jail to challenge the curfew order as discriminatory,
> endorsed restoration.of Selective Service because he felt it ended
> discrimination. Next they visited Amache to talk with confused
> young men being pressured by activists to resist military service.
> Then they traveled to Cheyenne, WY, to talk with some fifty
> imprisoned draft violators from the Heart Mountain camp. [To
> put the number of resisters in perspective, it should be noted that
> more than 700 men from Heart Mountain signed up for the draft

and took their physical examinations.] Some time later the pair
visited the Gila and Poston camps and patiently listened to the
protests of those opposing the draft. Their complaints had to do
mostly with bitterness over evacuation on the basis of race;
understandably they refused to serve in the uniform of a country
that had mistreated them.

Yasui and Masaoka agreed that the Evacuation was unjust,
but they also argued that the Nisei would be in a much stronger
position to demand justice if they demonstrated their loyalty by
complying with the draft law like all other citizens. By violating
the law, the two declared, the resisters were not only establishing
a criminal record for themselves, but taking an action that
reflected on the loyalty of all Japanese Americans. It is not likely
that the counseling did much good. The issue had become too
polarized for easy solution.

Although resisters were active in every camp, those in Heart
Mountain were the best organized. The leaders formed what they
called the Fair Play Committee and, citing Constitutional guarantees,
declared they would not report to draft boards for military service
until their rights were restored. The committee distributed a series of
press releases that were mostly ignored, except by Omura at the *Rocky
Shimpo*. In addition to publishing many stories about the committee
based on these releases, Omura commented vigorously in support of
the resistance movement in his "Know the Facts" column.

In April 1944 a Wyoming federal grand jury indicted seven lead-
ers of the Fair Play Committee and Omura on charges of "aiding and
abetting persons to evade registration or service in the land or naval
forces of the United States, and conspiracy." The seven were Kiyoshi
Okamoto, Paul Nakadate, Ben Wakaye, Frank Emi, Minoru Tamesa,
Sam Horino, and Guntaro Kubota. All except Omura were in Heart
Mountain and were charged with conspiracy to violate the Selective
Service Act and counseling others to resist the draft.

Another charge against the Heart Mountain Seven, as they came to be called, was that they transmitted to Omura "various articles and writing" that he printed in the *Rocky Shimpo*. Their case was heard in Cheyenne by U.S. district court judge T. Blake Kennedy and U.S. district court judge Eugene Rice.

In testimony at his trial Omura said he had no knowledge or information about the Fair Play Committee until he received letters from Okamoto and Nakadate in February 1944. He admitted that these letters, and other information he received from the committee, were used in news stories and as the basis for his comments in his "Know the Facts" column.

A random selection of his columns from this period reveals such statements as these:

The support we accord the Fair Play Committee at Heart Mountain is predicated simply upon our desire for authentic and authoritative clarification of the legal status of the Nisei as citizens.—April 7, 1944

We are as anxious as the Fair Play Committee to secure an authentic and authoritative legal clarification as to whether a citizen of the United States under technical suspension of his Constitutional guarantees would still be subject to the draft. No adequate reply has yet been delivered and in the meantime the Nisei-at-large are unnecessarily suffering while Washington remains silent.—April 3, 1944

What are the Nisei fighting for? Is he fighting to show the world that a Nisei is as good a soldier as the next one? I am sure he is not, basically. What he is fighting for is a principle. What he is fighting to preserve is a democratic way of life. What he is sacrificing his life for is the hope that America will restore those

inalienable rights that she so proudly claims to persons of
Japanese racial origin. It is therefore natural that in the absence of
any action on the part of the military and the federal government
to lift certain discriminatory restrictions pertaining to the U.S.
Japanese, that the Nisei should question the basic idea and
fundamental purpose of the Army in reinstituting draft proceedings.—February 11, 1944

The seven leaders of the Fair Play Committee were found guilty
of conspiracy to violate the Selective Service Act and counseling others to resist the draft, and sentenced to prison terms. But a year later
their convictions were overturned.

Regarding Omura, the court in instructions to the jury made
clear that the issue was whether Omura was "party to the conspiracy."
The court continued, "If after a fair and impartial consideration of
the evidence pertaining to the defendant Omura, you find that he
worked independently of the other defendants, you should find him
not guilty, even though you may find that he sought to accomplish
the same end as the other defendants sought to accomplish."

Omura was found not guilty, thus reaffirming press freedom to
cover the news and comment thereon. "I won the case," he remarked,
"but it left me flat broke." The *Rocky Shimpo* refused to take him back
and, unable to find another newspaper job, he worked as a landscape
gardener in Denver. Largely isolated from the Japanese American
community, he died in 1994.

As for Larry Tajiri, he decided he had had enough of ethnic journalism when JACL moved *Pacific Citizen* to Los Angeles after the
war. After a brief stint as managing editor of the *Free Press* in Colorado Springs, he joined the *Denver Post*. Given the assignment of
drama editor, he became one of the nation's most respected theater
critics. He died of heart problems at age fifty.

The entire matter of Japanese American draft resistance was badly muddled. In Arizona the federal judge presiding over the trial of 101 resisters from the Poston WRA camp found them guilty but fined them only one cent each. At Tule Lake the court dismissed charges against 26 resisters, finding it shocking that U.S. citizens being confined on suspicion of disloyalty should be compelled to serve in the armed forces. After the war President Harry Truman signed an executive order pardoning the resisters; 284 names were on the list.

War's end also brought significant changes to the Japanese American newspaper scene. The majority of evacuees hurried back to their West Coast homes where their communities were reborn and prewar newspapers resumed publication. With a dwindling local audience, *Rocky Shimpo* went out of business in 1951. *Colorado Times* lasted until 1962, its end hastened by a new paper, a four-page tabloid weekly called *Rocky Mountain Jiho,* which was started in 1961. One page was in English, edited on a part-time basis by Roy Takeno, who had studied journalism at the University of Southern California, and was devoted almost entirely to local community news.

The *Jiho*'s editor and publisher was Toshiro Tsubokawa, a veteran Japanese journalist. In his youth he had attended the University of Denver and taught Denver Nisei in the Japanese language school. And his wife, Sadako, was the daughter of Konai Miyamoto, a dentist prominent in the Denver Japanese community. Tsubokawa had returned to Japan after his studies at the University of Denver and joined *Yomiuri,* one of Japan's giant newspapers. At the time he retired and moved to Denver, he was chief of *Yomiuri*'s Washington bureau, a plum assignment.

The *Jiho* experienced financial difficulties from the very beginning, difficulties that continued even after the *Colorado Times* closed its doors in 1962. The community just was not big enough to support two papers and barely able to support one. There were not enough advertisers, and the number of people who could read or were interested in reading Japanese continued to dwindle.

Tsubokawa died unexpectedly in 1970. His widow struggled to keep the paper going but it was a losing proposition. She sold it in 1978 to a young immigrant couple from Japan, Eiichi and Yoriko Imada. Eiichi Imada had been a commercial and news photographer in Japan, and he and his wife were looking for an opportunity to settle in the United States. He has written of his experience: "They had no publishing experience and they knew that the *Jiho,* with its tiny circulation, with dim prospects of improvement, was a risky investment. Against the advice of friends, they decided to take over. In the beginning Issei women typesetters taught the amateur editors what they could about publishing a newspaper while leaving the English language page completely in Roy Takeno's hands."

The Imadas planned to try the publishing business for five years. They have survived for a quarter century and have become important members of Denver's Japanese American community.

chapter fourteen

THE SPECIAL PATRIOTS

Japanese Americans were not warmly welcomed in many parts of Colorado during World War II, but in at least two places they were considered an indispensable part of the national civilian war effort and treated accordingly. One was the University of Colorado campus in Boulder. The other was a suite of rooms in the since-demolished Albany Hotel located at Seventeenth and Stout Streets in downtown Denver.

The hotel housed radio station KFEL whose facilities were used by the secret Joint Anglo American Plan of Propaganda Projects for shortwave psychological warfare broadcasts beamed at Japan. Under this project, the British Political Warfare Mission (BPWM) and the American Office of War Information (OWI) used Nisei to write and broadcast news and commentary in Japanese to the ancestral land.

The Boulder campus from June 1942 until war's end housed the U.S. Navy Japanese Language School, which oddly enough had its beginnings in Tokyo. In 1905, after Japan's spectacular victory in the war against Russia, the U.S. defense establishment saw a need for learning more about the Japanese. The Army sent four officers to Tokyo in 1907 on a four-year assignment to learn the language. In 1910 the U.S. Navy established its own three-year language study program in Japan. The curriculum was developed by a Japanese named Naoe Naganuma who was to become famous for his teaching methods, which were widely adopted. In September 1941, as tension between the United States and Japan grew, the Navy closed its Tokyo school and sent the students home. It had graduated 48 officers, 35 of whom were available as language specialists when war broke out a few months later.

One of them was Albert E. Hindmarsh, a Japanese history scholar at Harvard and an officer in the Naval Reserve who early on had realized the importance of understanding the Japanese language. As Pacific tensions grew, he was instrumental in getting Japanese language crash courses started for Navy personnel at Harvard and the University of California at Berkeley. After the United States entered the war, the language program was concentrated at the University of California in Berkeley where the teachers were bilingual Japanese Americans.

The first director of the Navy's school in Berkeley was Florence Walne who had been born in Nagasaki to Baptist missionary parents and grew up completely bilingual. But the federal decision in early 1942 to move all Japanese Americans inland demolished her faculty making the program useless. Because of the program's intensive nature, there was one teacher for every five or six students, and Nisei were particularly valuable because they could explain difficult points of the Japanese language in English. Dr. Walne decided to follow her teachers inland and moved the school to Boulder where the University of Colorado had classroom space. She was the school's director until 1944 when she resigned because of poor health. Dr. Glenn Shaw, who had taught for twenty-five years in Japanese universities, was her successor.

The faculty of the Navy's Japanese language school was almost entirely Nisei—native-born Japanese Americans—with a few alien-born Japanese who were non-citizens because they were denied citizenship by law. Employment records show a total of 176 instructors over the school's four-year stay in Boulder, all but nine having Japanese names. After the move inland, recruiting qualified instructors was not easy. For many Nisei, Boulder was an unknown place and because they were not professionals, teaching a second language was a daunting challenge. Some of the best new teachers were recruited by other Nisei already on the Navy school staff who had taught Japanese in West Coast universities. One of them, Henry Tatsumi, a veteran of World War I who had pioneered teaching of the Japanese language at the University of Washington, invited several of his best former students to join the Boulder faculty. (The author, who had been a less than mediocre student in Tatsumi's classes, was not among the invited.)

Much of what follows in this chapter is based on the remarkably thorough research for a master's thesis by Jessica Natsuko Arontson of the University of Colorado and is utilized with deep appreciation and respect.

Arontson found that as language school enrollment grew, the school asked the *Colorado Times* in Denver to publish an item, translated as follows:

Search for Instructors

Urgently recruiting approximately 12 to 13 Issei and Nisei

As reported previously in this paper, the Japanese language school that was founded in Berkeley, California, with a student body consisting of future American diplomats as well as commissioned officers from the Army and Navy, will move to the University of Colorado at Boulder. According to plans, classes will begin on July 1. Nakamura Susumu, an instructor from the California school stopped for a brief visit to the city (Denver) the day before yesterday in order to recruit 12 to 13 Issei and Nisei to apply as instructors for the School.

Interested parties should inquire at the foreign languages department of the same school with the person in charge to discuss matters. No qualifications are necessary and educational history will not be considered. The salary is between 150 to 200 dollars. Interested parties should inquire at this newspaper's office in order to learn more about daily duties, regulations, and the procedure for written application.

One reason qualified Japanese Americans hesitated to apply was concern about how they would be treated in Boulder, an unknown destination. These were people who had been vilified by fellow citizens and exiled from West Coast homes by a suspicious and unsympathetic government. They knew that in Colorado the leading newspaper, the *Denver Post,* had been carrying on a shrill campaign against all Japanese Americans. Would they find acceptance in Boulder? Would Boulder citizens understand that they would be providing a critical war service that no one else could do?

Both the Navy and University of Colorado through university president Robert Stearnes and other prominent faculty leaders went to great lengths to educate Boulder citizens about the purpose of the Navy school and the important role of the Japanese American teachers. They gained the support of the city's newspaper, *The Daily Camera*. They talked to church and community leaders and real estate agents to help the instructors find housing. Generally, acceptance improved, but some of the teachers and their families reported being turned away at first by barbershops, beauty parlors, and apartment managers; denied service in restaurants; and taunted by children.

But at school the situation was different. In addition to Navy discipline and rigorous physical training, the students were required to adopt the strict Japanese ethic of respect for teachers. The teachers were not Mr. Yamada, but Yamada Sensei. The students—receiving intensive tutoring in subjects including written and spoken Japanese, Japanese history and customs—stood at attention when their teachers, entered the classrooms. The courses were difficult and fast-paced. For this instruction the students, who were enlisted men preparing for commissions as officers, were paid $21 a month plus room and board. One of the students, Roger Pineau, wrote of a humbling experience in *The Interpreter,* published by the University of Colorado's Archives:

> For the last day of our conversation class our *Sensei* had promised
> a sample of what we would experience in a war zone. We six
> stood as he entered our second floor classroom in the campus
> library that lovely, cool, June day. We exchanged *Ohayo*
> *gozaimasu* [formal Good Morning]. *Sensei* removed a Japanese
> newspaper from his briefcase, placed his pocket watch on the
> table, and began a 55-minute reading, without pause.
>
> We took this to be a challenge of what we had learned in 50
> weeks of concentrated effort—our concentration was intense.
> Within ten minutes I concluded that I was understanding only
> about one quarter of the reading, and sweat began seeping from
> every pore. When *Sensei* finished, he folded the paper into his

briefcase, pocketed his watch, wished us *Gokigenyo* [good luck] and departed. We sat there in a state of communal shock. We rose, moving out of the room and down the stairs, in a sort of zombie-like trance. I suppose we were all conjuring up the horror of being confronted with that kind of Japanese in a combat situation.

I was walking silently alongside Hy Kublin when we reached the open air. He stopped, turned to me, and declared, "Rog, if I were on a flagship and was summoned by the admiral to listen to a Japanese radio broadcast like that, I know just what I'd do." Because I was experiencing similar frightening scenarios, I implored, "Tell me, Hy, what would you do?"

Hy replied, "I'd sit down in front of the radio speaker, and listen intently for about half a minute. If what I heard was coming out like *Sensei's* reading, I'd stand up, look the admiral square in the eye and say, 'Sir, the dirty bastards have switched to Korean.'"

Royal Wald, another language school graduate, tells in *The Interpreter* of an experience he and another language school graduate, John A. Lacey, had in Shanghai after fighting ended but just before the formal Japanese surrender. Japanese warships were forbidden to leave but a destroyer captain attempted to take his ship down the river. He was apprehended, was brought back to face the ire of the U.S. commander, and gave some lame explanation. According to Wald, the U.S. commander angrily snapped, "Tell him that's chicken-shit." Wald could think only of a literal translation and as forcefully as he could he shouted the Japanese equivalent of "chicken defecation" while the Japanese captain tried to figure out what the bodily functions of a chicken had to do with the matter at hand.

Because of military secrecy, it is difficult to determine the exact number of graduates of the Navy's language school. As the war wound down Hindmarsh, by then a captain, reported that by March 1945, 684 individuals—573 male Navy officers, 111 Marine corps officers—plus 69 women in the WAVES had graduated from the Japanese language program. By June 1946 the number had increased to 801.

No doubt many of these individuals had no opportunity to use the Japanese language after the war and soon forgot what they had learned. But a few went on to careers involving Japan and the language. Jessica Arontson writes in her thesis:

The "Boulder Boys" as they came to be called, with their appreciation for the Japanese people gained at the JLS, on the battlefield pressed for civil treatment of Japanese prisoners of war. They also attempted to save Japanese soldiers and civilians on Okinawa and Iwo Jima by convincing them to surrender. One JLS soldier received an award for rescuing a Japanese unit from starvation due to bureaucratic neglect. Still close to their instructors and their experience in Boulder, JLS alumni acquired a sensitivity and admiration toward the Japanese people that followed them into war and impacted their decisions.

The furthest reaching legacy however involves what the students did at home upon returning from their wartime duties. After the war, many returned to graduate school with the intent to make Japan and Japanese culture their profession. Donald Keene ('43), Edward Seidensticker ('42), Helen Craig McCullough ('44), Thomas C. Smith ('43) and Roy Andrew Miller ('46) became internationally known scholars of Japanese literature, history, and linguistics.

Other JLS graduates who went into Asian studies include but are not limited to William T. DeBary ('43) University of Chicago; Frank Gibney ('43) Pacific Basin Institute, Pomona College; Soloman Levine ('43) University of Michigan; Roger Pineau ('43) Massachusetts Institute of Technology; Robert

Scalapino ('43) University of California at Berkeley; Donald Willis ('43) University of Colorado at Boulder; Ivan Morris ('44) Columbia University; Francis Hilary Conroy ('44) University of Pennsylvania; Sidney Brown ('45) University of Oklahoma.

Other graduates, Arontson reports, "went on to become foreign service or intelligence officers, academics, lawyers, politicians, business leaders and journalists. These former Japanese Language School students 'not only demystified Japan, they dispelled the vicious negative stereotypes of Japan by giving Americans an image based on deep knowledge of Japanese language and culture,' according to David Arase, a Pomona college professor and son of former JLS instructor Noboru Arase."

And it was Japanese American instructors who were responsible.

The United States Navy has acknowledged the school with a plaque that hangs in the Veterans Lounge of the University of Colorado Memorial Center. The plaque reads, "From 1942–1946, the U.S. Navy located its Japanese/Oriental Language School at the University of Colorado. Select students from throughout the U.S. participated in an immersion course taught mainly by Japanese American instructors. Upon graduation these men and women served in the Pacific Wars as Naval and Marine officer interpreters, interrogators, translators and cryptographers. After the War, many graduates became experts on Japan and Asia—translating the Far East for America on academic, intelligence and diplomatic levels."

The Navy language school was not widely publicized outside of Boulder, and the radio propaganda activity from Denver was even more hush-hush. The radio campaign's objective was to demoralize the Japanese by convincing them they were losing the war. In commentaries interspersed with nostalgic music, civilians in war zones were urged to surrender. There were news reports from combat areas that contradicted Japanese claims of victories. The broadcasts were beamed to combat areas as well as the Japanese homeland, but because Japanese civilians rarely had access to shortwave radio, the program's effectiveness is uncertain. (One estimate is that there may have been only 1,500 shortwave radios—many constructed secretly by amateur radio enthusiasts—in Japan.)

As many as twenty bilingual Nisei—some of them recruited from WRA camps—were employed by the radio projects during the war to write and broadcast the programs. Virtually all of them were Kibei—Nisei who had received part of their education in Japan—who were completely bilingual. They and their families lived normal if somewhat isolated lives in a city where the leading newspaper was waging a campaign against Japanese Americans. The radio program was so secret that not even the families of some broadcasters knew what they were doing.

Details of the program became public after another milestone in Japanese American history. In 1988 President Ronald Reagan signed the Civil Liberties Act, which, among other provisions, provided an official government apology for the injustice of the evacuation and payment of $20,000 for each survivor of that experience. Gary Ono of Simi Valley, California, and his brother, Victor, who had been born in Denver in 1944, wondered whether they were eligible. They weren't sure how their family happened to be in Denver after having been evacuated to the Granada camp. They began to ask some questions, which led them to Denver radio propaganda broadcasters who, until then, had been silent about their experiences. Fascinated, Gary Ono tracked down other participants of that project and put together a video documentary he titled "Calling Tokyo: Japanese American Radio Broadcasters During World War II," which premiered in 2002. (And, yes, the Ono brothers were eligible for survivor payments.)

chapter fifteen
AFTER THE WAR

The months after the Japanese surrender in September 1945 were, for Japanese American exiles from the West Coast, almost as stressful as the weeks that led to the evacuation. There were so many questions. Should we go back home? But back home to what? Where will we live? Our jobs and businesses are gone; how will we support our families until we get re-established? How will we be received by friends and people we did business with? Would we be smarter to stay where we are in places like Denver? And what is our future here?

The Japanese American Citizens League, which had been unable to block the evacuation but somehow survived the war years, now sought to establish a program to help their people cope with the future. Saburo Kido, the wartime president, spent long nights thinking about what should be done. His primary concern was to ensure that the wartime sacrifices of Japanese Americans—the civilians whose lives had been disrupted by forced relocation and the men who had fought and died for their country—must not have been in vain. A national convention would be necessary to present ideas for a post-war program to Japanese Americans. The most practical site—one that was central with a good mix of evacuees and unevacuated natives—was Denver. Kido asked the fledgling JACL chapter in Denver to host the meeting from February 28 to March 4, 1946, only six months after the war ended. Locals went to work—wartime newcomers to Denver like Min Yasui and his brother-in-law, Tosh Ando, along with Mits Kaneko, Roy Takeno, Bessie Matsuda, George Ohashi, George Furuta, Masako Takayoshi, Merijane Yokoe, Taki Domoto; natives like George Masunaga, Tak Terasaki and his wife, Michi, Dr. Tom Kobayashi and his wife, Haruko, Dr. Takashi Maeda and his wife, Bea; and a host of JACL leaders who had been scattered nationwide by the evacuation.

Kido presented a fourteen-point postwar agenda, many of which seemed impossible goals to the Denver gathering. They were the following:

(1) Naturalization and citizenship rights for all persons of demonstrated loyalty to the United States without regard to national origin, race or creed. [The Walter-McCarran Immigration and Naturalization Act of 1952 abolished the Oriental Exclusion Act of 1924 and eliminated race as a barrier to naturalization.]

(2) Reparations for the losses suffered by Japanese Americans in the Evacuation. [In summer 1988 Congress passed the Redress Bill under which the United States apologized for the injustice of the evacuation and gave $20,000 to each survivor.]

(3) Stay of deportation for Japanese nationals, primarily businessmen, stranded in the U.S. during the war. [Deportation
suspended.]

(4) Urging creation of a federal Department of Human Relations and Minority Problems. [Such a department has not
been created, but various movements have advanced the
rights of minorities.]

(5) The federal government should continue to discharge its
obligations to the evacuees. [The government has promoted
a new understanding of minority rights.]

(6) The constitutionality of alien land laws should be challenged
in the courts. [Alien land laws have been eliminated.]

(7) The constitutionality of the evacuation, specifically the basis
for arbitrary discrimination against one group of American
citizens, should be re-examined in the light of known facts
and without the pressure of wartime hysteria.

With regard to the seventh item, Congress named a blue ribbon commission in 1980 to, as President Jimmy Carter said, "expose clearly
what has happened in that period of war in our nation when many
loyal American citizens of Japanese descent were embarrassed during
a crucial time in our nation's history." The commission's report to
Congress in 1982 said in part:

> The promulgation of Executive Order 9066 was not justified by
> military necessity, and the decisions which followed from it—
> detention, ending detention and ending exclusion—were not
> driven by analysis of military conditions. The broad historical
> causes which shaped these decisions were race prejudice, war
> hysteria and a failure of political leadership. Widespread igno-
> rance of Japanese Americans contributed to a policy conceived in
> haste and executed in an atmosphere of fear and anger at Japan. A

grave injustice was done to American citizens and resident aliens of Japanese ancestry who, without individual review or any probative evidence against them, were excluded, removed and detained by the United States during World War II.

This report led to federal payments of $20,000 to each living evacuee (see Item 2 above).

(8) JACL should collect documents relating to the evacuation. [Undertaken in part by the Japanese American Research Project in cooperation with the University of California at Los Angeles.]

(9) Help Nisei veterans readjust to civilian life. [Done largely on a personal basis.]

(10) Keep the subject of Japanese Americans in the public eye until their problems are resolved. [An ongoing program.]

There were four other objectives concerned largely with internal matters.

Today, the Mile-Hi JACL chapter, as it is now called, is a small but active organization. Like the national Japanese American Citizens League, it has trouble maintaining membership as integration of Japanese Americans into the broader society proceeds steadily. A nucleus of younger Japanese Americans has largely replaced the original membership in Denver, but they have maintained their dedication to the organization's motto: Better Americans in a Greater America. The purpose of the organization's annual dinner to install a new cabinet has been expanded to include the Tom Masamori Kansha-no-hi ("Day of Thanksgiving") recognition to honor outstanding volunteers in community activities. Some members march in the annual Martin Luther King celebration and take part in other human rights activities not directly linked to Japanese Americans.

Faced with dwindling membership and income, the national organization, in the interest of economy, has abolished the Mountain-Plains District Council in which the Mile-High chapter was the largest and most active member. The Mile-High chapter has been absorbed into the Midwest District Council of which the Chicago chapter is the bellwether.

chapter sixteen

THE VETERANS

The bitter, bloody war between Japan and the United States came to an end on August 15, 1945. It was a day of elation and relief, and grief too that there had been so much bloodshed on both sides. For Coloradans with friends and family in the shattered islands, food, medicine, and clothing would be sent as soon as postal service resumed.

But the need turned out to be greater and more urgent than anyone imagined. Letters from Japan told of utter devastation, hunger, disease, hopelessness. At the end of November 1945, five and a half years after the prewar emergency meeting of Japanese leaders in the tri-states area, another meeting was called in Denver to organize a relief campaign. Various community organizations—churches and two Japanese language newspapers—and Japanese communities throughout Colorado, Nebraska, and Wyoming were represented by more than sixty delegates. Calling themselves the Tri-States Japan Relief Committee, they elected Dr. Konai Miyamoto and Ichiro Kaihara of the *Colorado Times* as their leaders and set out to solicit donations. Eventually $31,075 was collected—no small sum after the privation of the war years. After deducting expenses, $28,000 was sent to the American Friends Service Committee in Philadelphia, which was coordinating the U.S. overseas non-governmental relief effort.

In time the American Friends Service Committee reported that Denver's contribution had purchased 76,000 pounds of whole milk powder, 6,560 pounds of Pablum, 8,000 pounds of raisins, 433 pounds of miscellaneous medicines, and 10,075 pounds of sugar. The report also said $702 of Caprokol, a badly needed worm medicine, was ordered but had yet to be delivered.

At home, it was a time of waiting until their men in uniform—from occupied Europe, the far Pacific Islands, and Japan itself—would return to friends and family and start the difficult process of readjusting to civilian life.

For war veterans there would be much to forget and much to remember, and memories best shared over food and drink with those who had served in uniform. They found such a place in an American Legion Post, chartered May 31, 1946, by a handful of Chinese American veterans. Their headquarters were at 2015 Market Street in a two-story house where a Chinese family once had lived. The Chinese had named their organization Cathay American Legion Post 185 and, because their numbers were so limited, they invited Nisei veterans to join.

The Chinese link was no problem for the Nisei—after all they had been brothers in arms—but some were not enthusiastic about joining the American Legion. The Legion had been among the leaders in harassing Japanese Americans on the West Coast, especially in

California, both before and after Pearl Harbor. Many Nisei would have preferred to join the Veterans of Foreign Wars, but eventually some two hundred of them joined Cathay Post, which effectively became a Nisei post. Nisei Harry Shibao was the first commander, followed by James Nakagawa and John Noguchi. The new Nisei members were surprised to discover that the second floor of the Cathay Post building was a veritable casino. Many other veterans' clubs had been organized to run illegal but sanctioned gambling operations, but it was a relief to most of the Nisei when gambling was stopped after the city cracked down on such practices.

In spring 1946 the Nisei of Cathay Post became part of a much more proper activity. They were invited by the organizers of the Denver Memorial Day parade to put on their uniforms and march as a group. After the parade the Nisei vets drove out to Fairmount Cemetery and on a memorial site borrowed from the Veterans of Foreign Wars held a ceremony in remembrance of their buddies who hadn't come home.

This Memorial Day routine was followed for sixteen years. Then one day the Cathay Post chaplain, Rev. Paul Hagiya of the Simpson Methodist Church who himself was a veteran of military service, suggested at a meeting that it was time for the Nisei to have a memorial of their own. The problem was that Denver cemeteries were privately operated and, aside from Riverside, non-whites were still unwelcome—even in death.

A member of Cathay Post, Richard Shay, solved that problem. He rose to say, "I have just the place for you. If you like it, it's all yours." Shay was the executive secretary of the Fairmount Cemetery Association.

Shay offered to donate enough land for a monument and to make a number of burial sites around it available at cost. The offer was quickly accepted. In late 1962 John Noguchi, a veteran of military

service in the Pacific, and Yoshiaki Arai, a wounded veteran of service with the 442nd Regimental Combat Team in Europe, were
named co-chairmen of the Nisei War Memorial Project. One of their
first moves was to ask Floyd T. Tanaka, a 442nd veteran and architect employed as assistant executive director of the Denver Urban
Renewal Authority, to design a memorial. Meanwhile, they set out
to raise $20,000 in donations, a substantial amount in those days.

Tanaka's design, quickly adopted, consisted of five granite tablets, each six feet tall, standing in a row on a slightly elevated granite
base measuring 28 feet by 16 feet. Visitors could walk on the base to
read the messages cut into the stone.*

The first and second tablets in Tanaka's Denver monument are
titled "Freedom" and "Honor." The central tablet tells the story of
the memorial, and the fourth and fifth tablets are marked "Justice"
and "Equality." The names of the Nisei who made the ultimate sacrifice are chiseled into the four outer tablets.

The message on the front of the middle tablet reads, "Dedicated
in loving and timeless memory to our sons, fathers, husbands, brothers and friends who hesitated not to 'Go for Broke' in the nation's
defense, that we the beneficiaries of their sacrifice might enjoy without restriction our heritage as Americans." And under the message is
the following inscription: "Nisei War Memorial. Erected 1963 by
Comrades, Families, Friends in the Rocky Mountain Region and
American Legion Post 185."

On the reverse side of the middle tablet is the story of Japanese
Americans in military service: "Deeply aware the cloud of suspicion

---

*Many years later the Erickson Monument Company, which constructed
the monument, entered Tanaka's design in a national competition sponsored by the U.S. Naval Academy. It won, and a replica of the Denver monument now stands in Annapolis, Maryland.

Colorado's Japanese Americans who gave their lives in the nation's wars are commemorated at Denver's Fairmount Cemetery.

hanging over them in the early days of World War II could be dispersed only by a demonstration of loyalty, Americans of Japanese descent (Nisei) petitioned in 1942 for the right to serve their country. America offered them the opportunity and the Nisei served with distinction and valor in the 442nd Regimental Combat Team in Europe, in military intelligence units in the Pacific and elsewhere. More than 30,000 Nisei bore arms in World War II and Korea, shedding their blood on such far-flung battlefields as the Arno and Bruyeres, Guadalcanal, Myitkyina and Porkchop Hill. It is to those who made the supreme sacrifice in demonstrating that Americanism is not a matter of race or ancestry that this monument is dedicated."

This echoes the words of an unknown Nisei serviceman, who succinctly explained why he and his buddies performed so well. "We were fighting two wars—against the Fascist enemies of democracy, and to regain our rights as American citizens."

On the tablet marked "Freedom" are the names of these men: John Akimoto, Victor Akimoto, Yoshiharu Aoyama, Harry Hirao Endo, Abe Megumi Fuji, Teruo Ted Fujioka, George Futamata, Mitsuru Goto [K],* George Gushiken, Victor Katsumi Hada, John T. Hashimoto, Kanio Hattori, Stanley K. Hayama, Higuma Ikenouye, Masami Inatsu, Takashi Ito, Curtis Tadashi Ando [V], Kenneth B.K. Kozai [V], Higuma Ikegami [WWI], John Kimura, Haruto Moriguchi, Jimmie D. Nakayama [V], Masao Shigezani.

On the "Honor" tablet are the following names: John S. Kanazawa, Frank T. Kanda, Jero Kanetomi, James S. Karatsu, Haruo Kawamoto, George Y. Kawano, Cike C. Kawano, Matsuo Kenmotsu, Yasuo Kenmotsu, Leo Kikuchi, Paul T. Kimura, Mamoru Kinoshita, Roy Joseph Kitagawa, James Toshio Kokubu, John Kyono, Eso Masuda, Peter Masuoka, Michio Matoba [K], George M. Mayeda, Joseph H. Morishige, Kiyoshi R. Muranaga, James Nagata, Masao Nakagaki, Kongo Nitta, Michiyasu Matoba.

The "Justice" tablet lists the following men: Arnold Ohki, John T. Okada, Susumu Okura, Katsu Okida, George Omokawa, Lloyd M. Onoye, Robert Z. Ozaki, George Saito, Calvin Saito, Yoshinori Sakai, Masa Sakamoto, Tadao Sakohira, George S. Sameshima, Toll Seiki, Kenneth Kentaro Shibata, James Kiyoshi Shiramizu, Masao Shigezane, George M. Shimada, Toshiaki Shoji, Sadamu R. Sueka, Bob Sueoka, Wesley Shimoda (V).

And on the "Equality" tablet are the following names: Shigeo Tabuchi, Cooper Tahara, William Taketa, Tadashi T. Takeuchi, Kei

*"K" signifies service in the Korean War, "V" signifies the Vietnam War, and "WWI" signifies World War I. All others served in World War II.

Tanahashi, Harley Tanaka, John Y. Tanaka, Saburo Tanamachi, Harry Tokushima, Haruo Tomita, Ryuichi Watada (K), Bill Iwao Yamaji, Fred Yamashita, Joe R. Yasuda, Mitsuru Yeto, Hitoshi Yonemura, Shiyoji Yunoki.

This memorial commemorates a staggering number of men killed in action from one community, but mercifully most came home unscathed and had interesting stories to tell. A few of those stories are recounted here.

Nobuo Furuiye, born in Lafayette, Colorado, was among those sent to the Japanese language school at Camp Savage in Minnesota. He was attached to a Canadian artillery unit in the Kiska campaign in the Aleutians. Under attack by Allied forces the Japanese fled under cover of dense fog, leaving behind sacks of rice, kegs of soy sauce, and many cases of canned food. Furuiye recalls that he urged that the food be sent to Japanese Americans in relocation camps instead of being destroyed. Apparently this was done.

After the Aleutians campaign, Furuiye was among the Nisei attached to an Army intelligence unit in Hawaii. Assigned one day to deliver some secret documents to Naval headquarters at Pearl Harbor, he was denied entry at the security gate because of his race. Later he was sent to examine captured documents in places like Tarawa, Saipan, and Guam. In the final days of the war he waded ashore with the Marines in the bloody battle for Iwo Jima and was wounded. Despite his service, he was not awarded the Purple Heart Medal that he deserved until years later. It was explained that because the Marines did not carry Furuiye on their roster and the Army was unaware of his wounds, he was not reported as a casualty. Long after the war the oversight was brought to official attention by his Denver friend, retired Maj. Gen. Henry Larson, and rectified. Immediately after Japan surrendered, Furuiye was flown to Kyushu to work with the

Naval Technical Mission to inventory captured weapons. During the Korean War he was recalled to duty and assigned to teach Japanese at the Defense Language School in Monterey, California.

Sueo Ito, who became a dentist after the war, worked in Japan and then the Philippines on translation teams for the trials of Gen. Masayuki Yamashita, known as the Tiger of Malaya, and Gen. Masaru Homma, commander of Japanese troops at the time of the Bataan death march. Both generals were found guilty and executed. Ito, reassigned to Japan, then served as interpreter in the trial of an American colonel who was convicted of stealing more than five hundred precious stones from a Japanese bank vault.

The experience of Nebraska-born Albert Kushihashi was a prime example of the way racial discrimination hurt the war effort. Even before graduation from high school he took flying lessons, and in 1937 he received his flight instructor's certificate. Despite the desperate need for pilots, Kushihashi was shunted off to teach Japanese—a job that he was not qualified for. When the war in Europe ended in spring 1945 Kushihashi was sent to Fort Benning, Georgia, where he was required to wear Japanese military uniform and pose as the enemy to help train young officers destined for the Pacific.

The men in the Hawaiian Nisei 100th Battalion and the 442nd Regimental Combat Team, which later absorbed the 100th, suffered so many casualties in Italy and France that it was called the Purple Heart regiment. Their heroics won them 18,140 individual decorations, including nearly 9,500 Purple Heart medals for battle wounds with 680 killed in action. Among the decorations were more than 4,000 Bronze Star Medals and 1,200 Oak Leaf Clusters in lieu of second Bronze Stars, 560 Silver Stars and 268 Oak Leaf Clusters in lieu of a second Silver Star, 52 Distinguished Crosses, and one Medal of Honor. That went to Pfc. Sadao S. Munemori, a Californian who had given his life to save some of his comrades in a battle in Italy.* Late in 1945, when the 442nd was waiting to come home, the Army newspaper *Stars and Stripes* reported that seven unnamed Nisei soldiers had been recommended for the Medal of Honor but none were approved.

Decades after the end of World War II, questions began to be raised about why Japanese Americans had been awarded fifty-two Distinguished Service Cross medals, but only one Medal of Honor. Had racial discrimination been involved even on the battlefield? Early in 1996 President Clinton signed a bill requiring that each Distinguished Service Cross and Navy Cross award made during World War II to Asian Americans, Native Americans, or Pacific Islanders be reviewed "to determine whether any such award should be upgraded to the Medal of Honor." In summer 2000, fifty-five years after war ended, President Clinton in a glittering White House ceremony awarded the nation's highest military honor for bravery to twenty Japanese Americans, one Chinese American, and one Filipino American who previously had received lesser awards. Only seven were still alive to accept the Medal of Honor in person. One was Daniel K. Inouye, U.S. senator from Hawaii. Another was an unassuming Denver postal worker, George (Joe) Sakato.

Born in Colton, California, east of Los Angeles, where his family ran a barbershop and pool hall, Sakato and his family had moved to Phoenix to avoid the evacuation. Sakato lost thirty-five pounds picking cantaloupes in the Arizona sun, worked in a grocery store, and then volunteered for the Air Force. Instead of the Air Force, he found himself at Camp Shelby in the Mississippi bottomlands being trained

---

*The second Nisei to be awarded a Medal of Honor was Sgt. Hershey Miyamura of Gallup, New Mexico, for heroism in the Korean War.

Joe Sakato, retired postal worker, belatedly receives the Congressional Medal of Honor from President Clinton for extraordinary bravery during World War II.

as a replacement in the Nisei 442nd Regimental Combat Team, which was taking heavy casualties in Italy.

Sakato, assigned to E Company of the 442nd, soon found himself in the Vosges Mountains of southern France. On October 29, 1944, he was severely wounded and hospitalized for seven months. Unknown to Joe, his commanding officer had recommended him for a medal. He learned of the Distinguished Service Cross award on March 23, 1945, as he was preparing for discharge.

The hospital staff wanted to stage a parade in Sakato's honor but he declined. "Just send me the medal," he said. He was thinking of his squad leader who had been hit in the skirmish and died in Joe's arms. Sakato took his discharge and came to Denver where some of his family had settled. He worked as a diesel mechanic, married Boulder-born Bess Saito, then joined the U.S. Postal Service where he worked until retirement.

Sakato, of course, was pleased to hear about the Medal of Honor but far from excited. The war had been so long ago. The notice said the medal would be awarded by the president in a ceremony in the Rose Garden of the White House and because of limited space only ten seats would be allotted to each recipient. That wasn't nearly enough to take care of Joe's family and some of the buddies who had survived the action for which he was being recognized. "Thanks, but I can't come," he notified the White House. "Just mail me the medal."

Fortunately, Sakato was able to receive his medal in person. A huge circus tent had been erected on the White House grounds for another function and was kept in place for the Medal of Honor ceremony. Thirty-four of Joe's family and friends attended the award ceremony where the Medal of Honor was presented by President Clinton in the name of Congress to Pvt. George T. Sakato "for conspicuous gallantry and intrepidity at the risk of his life above and beyond the call of duty." It said further:

> Private George T. Sakato distinguished himself by extraordinary heroism in action on 29 October 1944, on hill 617 in the vicinity of Biffontaine, France. After his platoon had virtually destroyed two enemy defense lines, during which he personally killed five enemy soldiers and captured four, his unit was pinned down by heavy enemy fire. Disregarding the enemy fire, Private Sakato made a one-man rush that encouraged his platoon to charge and destroy the enemy strongpoint. While his platoon was reorganizing, he proved to be the inspiration of his squad in halting a counter-attack on the left flank during which his squad leader was killed. Taking charge of the squad, he continued his relentless tactics, using an enemy rifle and P-38 pistol to stop an organized enemy attack. During this entire action, he killed 12 and wounded two, personally captured four and assisted his platoon in taking 34 prisoners. By continuously ignoring enemy fire, and

by his gallant courage and fighting spirit, he turned impending
defeat into victory and helped his platoon complete its mission.
Private Sakato's extraordinary heroism and devotion to duty are
in keeping with the highest traditions of military service and
reflect great credit on him, his unit, and the United States Army.

The citation was signed, "William J. Clinton."

Among those who witnessed the ceremony was Sakato's brother-
in-law, Carl Saito, who had performed heroically in a battle near
Bruyers, France. Saito was an unarmed litter-bearer taking a wounded
G.I. back to an aid station when the Nazis captured him. He spent
seven months in a prisoner of war camp near Munich, surviving on a
bread and water diet, before the war ended. He came home to the
family farm near Henderson and eventually worked as an electronics
supervisor at the Martin Marietta plant.

Although only a few of the Nisei heroes could be recognized and
honored, there seemed to be a need to express the community's thanks
to the thousands of nameless "dogfaces" who had stepped forward
and served a country they believed in despite its betrayal. That tribute
appeared in my column, called "From the Frying Pan," which appeared in the September. 14, 1984, issue of *Pacific Citizen*, the publication of the Japanese American Citizens League.

The occasion that inspired the column was the opening of the
Nisei Legion Post's "Go for Broke" photo exhibit commemorating
their sacrifices in the war. The column said in part:

> We Japanese Americans owe an enormous debt of gratitude to
> the guys who had faith enough in our country to swallow the
> humiliation of evacuation and incarceration to volunteer for
> military service. It is not overly dramatic to say that they wrote
> the message of Japanese-American loyalty with their blood and all
> of us are beneficiaries of their sacrifice.

Many of those who volunteered for service were under enormous hostile pressure from peers who saw neither wisdom nor logic in fighting for a nation that had betrayed them. There was much that was persuasive in the argument that the U.S. should do right by Japanese Americans before they agreed to fight for it. But the Nisei volunteers, and the draftees who followed them, laid down no preconditions. That was not the time for bargaining. It was unfair that they should have to demonstrate a loyalty that should have been obvious, loyalty that should have been assumed. But that was not the way it was. And so these fellows who have grown into old soldiers, shook off the jeers and the hostility of those of lesser faith, were bloodied in battle, lost good buddies, and it is only proper that we should commemorate what they experienced.

Old soldiers, indeed. That is a description that they can accept and proudly wear as a badge of respect, admiration and affection.

Meanwhile, as membership in the Legion Post (whose name was changed to Nisei Post in 1982) dwindled, there was concern about what eventually would happen to the property that, like the Japanese Association's lot in the same area, had appreciated hugely in value—more than $1.5 million according to some estimates. At a memorable meeting in January 2000, the Nisei Post unanimously adopted a measure, proposed by Yosh Arai, making sure that no member, past or present, would benefit from the property if and when the building and land were to be sold. The veterans set up a nonprofit Nisei Veterans Heritage Foundation and John Noguchi as president of Nisei Post 185 signed a quitclaim deed granting the property to the new foundation. Veterans now have use of the property and income from Mori's, a sushi restaurant that leases the kitchen and dining room.

chapter seventeen

SAKURA SQUARE

The heart of Denver's Japantown, Nineteenth to Twentieth Streets and Larimer to Lawrence, and the surrounding area grew shabbier as the years passed. By 1962 the lay leaders of the Denver Buddhist Temple, which was near the corner of Twentieth and Lawrence, realized they needed to improve the site. But how? They also wanted to sponsor a low rent housing project for the growing number of elderly in the community, with or without the cooperation of the Japanese Association, which also was considering a housing project.

The problem came to a head four years later when the Denver Urban Renewal Authority (DURA) announced it was preparing to demolish the outdated structures on thirty square blocks of lower downtown Denver and open the property for rebuilding a modern city district. The Buddhist Temple was at the edge of this project. Members were told they could sell their building and move out of the area, or buy and develop the entire block—Nineteenth to Twentieth, Larimer to Lawrence—after it was cleared of all but the temple.

It was an opportunity and challenge on a scale never experienced by the Japanese American community. Fortunately, government projects progress slowly, providing the temple leaders time to weigh the opportunities as well as the burdens associated with redeveloping an entire city block. Finally, on March 10, 1971, the Tri-States Buddhist Church purchased the property from DURA for $188,800 to build what would be called the Sakura ("Cherry Blossom") Square project.

A plan evolved to build a 20-story apartment building that would be called Tamai Tower. It would be the tallest building in the area, with 204 apartments plus a community room on the top floor. The first two levels were to be commercial. A strategic ground-floor corner of the tower was spoken for by the Granada market. Adjoining the tower and linked to it by an overpass would be a two-story commercial complex. A large plaza designed like a Japanese garden, located near the tower's entrance, would carry an identifying sign— Sakura Square—in English and Japanese script. Only a few decades earlier Japanese bathhouses had occupied the site. The board that made the decision to take on the project was made up of Tsunoda, Ben Hara, Jim Kanemoto, Floyd Koshio, Lee Murata, Edward Nakagawa, Frank Nakata, Sam Suekama, Jim Tochihara, A. M. Watada, Kenzo Fujimori, and Herb Inouye—all but two of them Nisei.

Bruton Bertram and Associates were the architects and Titan Construction Company became the contractors. With a forty-year loan guarantee from the Federal Housing Administration, the First National Bank of Denver provided a construction loan of $3,907,000 and the Metropolitan Life Insurance Company provided an extended loan of $4,023,800. It was by far the most ambitious project undertaken by the Denver Japanese American community. Ground was broken March 17, 1971. The topping out ceremony for the Tamai Tower residential section was held January 25, 1972, with a proper Buddhist ceremony in which, incongruously but appropriately, Tamai, Tsunoda, and Unryu Sugiyama wore construction workers' hard hats as they recited the sutra.

Just a little over two years after construction began, on the weekends of May 12–13 and May 19–20, 1973, Tamai Tower and Sakura Square were dedicated at ceremonies attended by, among others, Colorado governor John Vanderhoof, Denver mayor Bill McNichols, and Bishop Kenryu Tsuji of the Buddhist Churches of America. Tamai Tower's first administrator was Floyd Koshio of Fort Lupton and his wife Ina served as office manager. Kenzo Fujimori later joined the staff as co-administrator.

The original business firms leasing space in the project were Pacific Mercantile, Granada Supermarket, Sakura Beauty Salon, Nakai's Gift Shop, Haws and Company, which retailed Asian antiques and art goods, and two restaurants.

One was the Akebono Restaurant owned by Fred Aoki. He moved his restaurant from the pool hall on Larimer across the street into spanking new quarters on the second floor of the tower. The other restaurant was a tastefully designed place called the Kyoto with a fine bar and tatami rooms for an upscale clientele. It was owned by a young international businessman named Hirosuke Ishikawa who had built up a lucrative transportation empire—taxis, busses, trucking—in Japan. Ishikawa had been a principal investor in a fledging Denver life insurance company called United Nations Life, which had been supported by the Buddhist Temple. When the company was in trouble, he sent one of his young aides, Seiji Tanaka, to take on the impossible task of saving United Nations Life. When Ishikawa was persuaded to finance a first-class restaurant in Sakura Square, he assigned Tanaka the job of manager, and for many years the Kyoto with its bevy of kimono-clad waitresses was a prime attraction.

Today only Pacific Mercantile and the Haws Company remain of the original tenants. The Sakura Beauty Salon has been taken over by the Nonakas. Mas Nonaka, whose mother once operated a barbershop on Larimer Street, takes care of the masculine trade and his wife, Yasuko, operates the beauty parlor. Among the new tenants are a dental clinic, the M.E.M. Travel Bureau, Yoko's Japanese fast-food restaurant, the *Rocky Mountain Jiho* newspaper, Eiichi Imada's Japan Consultants Office, offices of the Japanese Association, and the Museum of Contemporary Art in the space the Granada market once occupied.

At first elderly Japanese were reluctant to abandon their homes for a high-rise tower, but that changed when the early tenants spread the word about the convenience, comfort, and security of apartment living. One of them was Tamai himself. Today Tamai Tower is a relaxed, cheerful multiethnic community, and a long, long way from the ramshackle building where the priest had a leaky-ceilinged bedroom when he first came to Denver.

Over the years Sakura Square has become the center of Denver Japanese American activity. The temple's auditorium and gymnasium are in frequent use. Because spring weather in Colorado is capricious, the Cherry Blossom Festival is celebrated each summer and Lawrence Street is blocked off between Nineteenth and Twentieth for this street fair that brings out thousands.

The Japanese garden in Sakura Square is an island of tranquility, the quiet broken at times by the clamor of schoolchildren visiting this tiny piece of Japan. The garden, designed for peaceful viewing and

*As governor of Colorado, Ralph Carr sacrificed his political
career to stand up for justice for Japanese Americans.*

contemplation, was created by the Japanese Gardeners Association;
plantings were donated by Tawara Nurseries. It also features memo-
rials to three individuals who have meant much to the Japanese Americans (see Chapter 10).

The first is a bust of Governor Ralph Carr, who never wavered in
his outspoken support for Japanese American rights.

In 1990 the community installed a bust of Minoru Yasui, a community leader and civil rights activist who is described on the memorial as "An American of Uncommon Courage and Principle." Yasui
was born in Hood River, Oregon, in 1916 and died in Denver on
November 12, 1986. He was one of four Japanese Americans who

went to court early during World War II to challenge the legality of federal measures restricting the rights and freedoms of Japanese Americans. Engraved on the granite pedestal are these words:

> So fervently did Minoru Yasui believe in the rights guaranteed by the Constitution that during World War II he endured nine months of solitary confinement to test the government's authority to discriminate against Americans of Japanese ancestry on the basis of race. The U.S. Supreme Court ruled against him, but Yasui ultimately was vindicated when the 100th Congress and President Ronald Reagan apologized to Japanese Americans for the injustice of suspended freedoms. As director of Denver's Commission on Community Relations, Yasui dedicated his life to advancing the rights of his fellow man regardless of color or creed. This monument is dedicated to the memory of an uncommon American who served his nation with extraordinary commitment to its highest principles.

Yasui's memory also is honored by the Minoru Yasui Community Award, administered by the Denver Foundation, which makes contributions to public service organizations in the name of outstanding community volunteers.

The third memorial is a near life-size statue of Tamai, the beloved priest who was born October 10, 1900, and died September 25, 1983. A plaque explains:

> A native of Toyama-ken, Japan, Tamai came to Denver in June of 1930. He devoted the rest of his life—53 years—to the spiritual, cultural and social needs of Buddhists in Colorado, Wyoming, Nebraska, Montana, Kansas, Oklahoma, Texas and New Mexico. He taught by example those admirable qualities embodied in the Buddhist faith. His kindness and compassion touched thousands, creating a rich and lasting heritage. Tamai Tower was erected in

1972 as a living memorial to this gentle priest recognized as one of Jodo Shinshu's most eminent ministers. This statue is dedicated to his memory by a community which loved and respected the priest often called the "Living Buddha." Dedicated October 5, 1996.

chapter eighteen
SISTER CITIES

One day in summer 1960 Tamotsu Murayama of the *Japan Times,*
Japan's leading English language newspaper, called on me in my office at the *Denver Post*. I had known Murayama since before the war
when he worked on Japanese language newspapers in San Francisco,
but he had spent the war years in Japan. He said he had come to
Colorado as the leader of a delegation of Japanese Boy Scouts attending a world jamboree near Colorado Springs. But he had come to see
me on another mission.

"Would Denver consider becoming a sister city with Takayama,
a mountain community in central Japan?" he asked.

The sister cities movement to promote international friendship
and understanding had been launched by President Dwight D.
Eisenhower only a short time earlier. Denver already had one sister
city, Brest, France. This relationship had been established indepen-

dently soon after World War II ended, when France was in dire straits.

I responded to Maruyama's query with another question. "Where in central Japan? Never heard of Takayama."

Murayama explained that Takayama was a community of perhaps 65,000 in the mountains inland from Nagoya, Japan's third largest city. It had many ancient temples and shrines and was known as the second Kyoto. It was probably too small a target to be bombed by the Americans during the war, so it was unscathed. Like Denver, it was a tourist destination, with sightseeing and festivals in the warm months, skiing in winter, and plenty of hot springs year-round in which to soak away aches and pains. He also explained that although Takayama was unfamiliar with Denver, it had been recommended as a possible sister city by the postmaster at Nagoya because of the many similarities.

I expressed skepticism. "Denver is almost ten times as big as your town and nobody knows where Takayama is," I said. "Don't know whether there's any interest here. Let's go find out."

We walked to Denver mayor Dick Batterton's office in City Hall where Murayama explained his mission. Batterton listened intently. He could have said he would like to talk to some citizens about the invitation. He was not known for hasty decisions. He could have said he wanted to think about it and find out what the obligations would be. What he did say was: "Sounds like a good idea. Let's go ahead."

Then he walked to an outer room, summoned the press, and announced that Denver and Takayama, Japan, were about to become sister cities. Next day the *Denver Post* published a photograph of Murayama in his Boy Scout shorts, showing Batterton pictures of Takayama. The proclamation Batterton signed read:

> Whereas, the city of Takayama, Japan, has asked to be affiliated as
> a "sister city" under the program of international good will

proposed by the Department of State of the United States of America; and

Whereas, Takayama is situated in a mountainous region in the central part of Japan, and has a background and tradition in many ways comparable to ours; and

Whereas, since this is the centennial year of the Treaty of Amity and Commerce between Japan and the United States, such a fraternal tie would be most timely; and

Whereas, such an affiliation would in no way affect the association we now enjoy with Brest, France, save to complement and give added significance to Denver's efforts to promote international understanding and goodwill;

Now, therefore, I, Richard Y. Batterton, Mayor of the City and County of Denver, Colorado, do proclaim that Takayama, Japan, and Denver, Colorado, U.S.A., are "Sister-Cities," and call upon all citizens of Denver to recognize this voluntary tie of friendship with the people of Takayama and take every opportunity to foster a close relationship between the two cities.

In witness thereof, I hereunto set my hand and have caused the seal of the City of Denver to be affixed this 29th day of July, 1960.

Several weeks later, Benjamin F. Stapleton III, a Denver attorney who was the honorary consul of France for Colorado and was in Asia with some thirty Colorado high school students under an American Field Service exchange program, astonished Takayama's city hall by dropping by to say howdy.

That was the beginning of a remarkably warm and active friendship—shared by business and political leaders, educators, students, and ordinary people—that has flourished for nearly half a century.

In spring 1961 Mrs. Elizabeth Rose, who had become chairperson of the Denver-Takayama Sister Cities Committee, visited Takayama for the first time. A few months later Shuzo Tsuchikawa, former mayor of Takayama, visited Denver. The following year Mrs. Rose went to Takayama again with a group of Denver Boy Scouts who delivered hundreds of books about the United States, which were distributed to schools and placed in a "Denver Room" in the Takayama library. In 1977 Mrs. Rose was decorated by the government of Japan with the Third Order of the Precious Crown, Butterfly, in recognition of her service with UNESCO, including helping to found United Nations University in Japan.

In August 1964 Mayor Shinichiro Iwamoto led a group of twenty men to the United States to celebrate what was publicized as Denver's Takayama Festival. From Takayama a colorful, full-size, medieval float—like those pulled through the streets in Takayama's famous festival parades—had been disassembled, shipped to San Francisco, and then trucked to Denver (thanks to Frank Torizawa's good auspices) where it was re-assembled by craftsmen. Even in America no celebration would be complete without a parade. Some local Japanese Americans were outfitted in medieval Japanese costumes and, to the deep boom-boom of drums and the shrill accompaniment of fifes, they hauled the float majestically from Broadway down Sixteenth Street, across California Street to Fifteenth, and back up to Civic Center where the visitors performed colorful Takayama folk dances. Later, in an open field ceremony at the edge of the Botanic Gardens, a massive stone lantern from Takayama was presented to the city. The stone lantern now stands at the entrance to the Japanese garden at the west end of the Botanic Gardens. Since then a modest Takayama Memorial Park was built on Cherry Creek Drive and a Denver Park built in Takayama.

Another memorial to this partnership is the float from Takayama. As colorful and impressive as the float was, it later proved to be a problem for the city of Denver because of its size. At first it was

displayed on the ground floor of City Hall, then because it was im-
peding foot traffic the float was moved to the first floor of the Stapleton
Airport lobby. Next the float was moved to the Forney vintage car
and transportation museum in a cavernous old building near the Platte
River. Ultimately the float found a home in Sakura Square where it is
displayed under the overhang of the commercial wing in a huge glass
enclosure paid for by the Sakura Square management and contributions
from members of the Denver-Takayama Sister Cities committee.

Individual Denverites and small groups (including the University of Denver jazz band in 1965) had visited Takayama, but the first
official call was made in 1966 by Mayor Tom Currigan leading a
delegation of forty-nine civic and business leaders. They were entertained royally. The visit was a huge success as could be surmised from
a photograph published by the Japanese media showing a grinning
Currigan up to his neck in a hot springs pool with a folded towel on
his head, Japanese-style.

A series of art and cultural exchanges followed. Paintings and
woodblock prints by Takayama students were displayed in Denver.
The Cherry Creek Senior High School in suburban Denver sent its
thirty-member Meistersingers to Takayama where they performed
with the Takayama Citizens Chorus and high school bands.

In July 1976 a goodwill delegation of forty, led by Vice-Mayor
Ryoichi Yamada, came to Denver to participate in the American Bi-
centennial and the State of Colorado's centennial celebrations. While
Takayama men and women dressed in summer *yukata* danced along
the parade route, Yamada rode in an open limousine waving to spec-
tators like any American politician. Two years later Mayor Kichiro
Hirata led another delegation to Denver. While members of his party
were sightseeing in the Rockies, Mayor Hirata impressed his Denver
hosts by asking to skip the tour and visit the city sewage disposal

plant instead. He explained that Takayama was preparing to install a modern sewage disposal system and he wanted to learn how an American city served its citizens.

Music also linked the two cities as Denverites were surprised, and pleased, to learn that Takayama had a modern concert hall, several choral groups that sang both Western and Japanese pieces with great verve and feeling, and an excellent wind orchestra. The orchestra, its members paying their own way to Denver, played before packed houses on several occasions, sometimes making music with musicians from the Denver Municipal Band, the Colorado Wind Ensemble, Denver Concert Band, and Rocky Mountain Brass.

Despite its casual beginnings, the success of the Denver-Takayama sister cities relationship—it won two Reader's Digest Foundation Awards—can be credited largely to dedicated leadership on both sides of the Pacific. In Denver, after Elizabeth Rose helped lay the groundwork, Miriam Haley, wife of a prominent physician, took over the presidency of the Denver-Takayama Committee. She was followed by businessperson Lindy Barker then Dr. Ayako Wada, the Japan-educated Nisei physician and wife of Colorado native Dr. Takashi Mayeda. Dr. Wada headed the Denver-Takayama committee for more than a decade before handing the reins to Teddie Nead, a city employee who became interested after escorting a delegation of physically handicapped Denverites to Takayama in 1981 as part of the International Year of Disabled Persons observance. That project was followed by a reciprocal visit to Denver by a group of young handicapped persons from Takayama.

Teddie Nead, whose surname became Throm after her marriage, was succeeded by Kitty Comstock who in turn was succeeded by the dynamic Kimiko Side. Born in Beijing of Japanese parents, Mrs. Side spent the war years in Tsingtao in North China, where her father was a pharmacist. The family was repatriated after the war and she was working in a Tokyo bank when she met Gene Side, an American serviceman on occupation duty. They were married in 1951 and moved to Denver in 1958.

While helping her husband start a now-thriving business of importing and exporting novelties, Mrs. Side channeled her energy into supporting the Japanese American community's numerous activities. The Sides have been generous about opening their home for garden parties and receptions for Takayama visitors. She has supported both the Simpson Methodist Church and the Denver Buddhist Temple with craft classes and served two terms as president of the Japanese Association.

The Japanese side has enjoyed similarly dedicated leadership, starting with Mayor Shinichiro Iwamoto who headed the first delegation to Denver. Presidents of the Takayama/Denver Friendship Association have been Dr. Masatoshi Murata, Yukio Hirata, Dr. Akira Hisakane, and currently Tadao Shimohata. Education has been an important part of the Denver-Takayama relationship. Seventeen Denver-area high school students visited Takayama in summer 1983. Twenty Takayama high school students visited Denver the following year, and in 1985 Denver sent fourteen students to Takayama. This student exchange remains an important part of the Denver-Takayama relationship. Home stays play a key role in the cross-cultural experience for students from both countries.

Three other Colorado cities, and the State of Colorado itself, have established long-lasting "sister" relations with Japanese counterparts. All of these ties began as casually as the Denver-Takayama relationship, and Elizabeth Rose had a role in one of them.

On her trip to Japan in 1961 to firm up the Denver-Takayama arrangement, she happened to meet the mayor of Fujiyoshida, a famous resort and outdoors recreation center near the foot of Mount Fuji. When she learned Fujiyoshida was looking for an American sister city, Mrs. Rose suggested an ideal candidate—Colorado Springs. Like Fujiyoshida, Colorado Springs was near the foot of a famous mountain—Pikes Peak—and tourism was a major industry. And besides a lot of nice people lived there, including a number of Japanese women married to U.S. servicemen who had been rotated to nearby military installations and were now retired in the area. The upshot was that Fujiyoshida enthusiasts suggested to Colorado Springs officials that they study the possibility of becoming sister cities. It did not take long. On February 13, 1962, the Colorado Springs city council adopted a resolution approving the relationship. Two months later at a meeting of interested citizens William Vandel was named chairman. A monument to the Colorado Springs-Fujiyoshida relationship is a *torii*—a log gate that stands at the entrance to a shrine or temple— installed near downtown in the parkway on a main north-south street in the central area.

In addition to the usual citizen visits, the two cities have had notable success with a middle school exchange program. Four Fujiyoshida middle schools send four students each to Colorado Springs each summer along with two chaperones for five to seven days of homestays with American families that have children of about the same age. Madolia Massey Mills, director of the Fujiyoshida Committee, says the visitors are exposed to daily life with the American host families—grocery shopping, participating in sports, visiting schools and shopping malls, as well as taking in tourist attractions and Native American sites. E-mail allows the participants to maintain their new friendships even after they return home.

Thanks to the generous contribution of time and effort by Lt. Col. Paul Maruyama, Colorado Springs is also closely involved in

Japan's Manjiro International Exchange Program. Founded in Japan, this grass roots effort is named for the humble Japanese fisherman who was rescued from a tiny Pacific island and brought to America in 1843. Its objective is closer relations between Japanese and Americans. Two Colorado Springs mayors—Robert Isaacs and Mary Lou Makepeace—have visited Japan under this program. Civic leader Tom James is the volunteer head of the Manjiro program's Center for International Exchange U.S., which has a small office donated by the El Pomar Foundation.

Denver is also the home of the Japan America Society of Colorado, one affiliate of a nationwide group headquartered in Washington, D.C., whose main objective is to promote cultural understanding between the people of the two countries and, incidentally, to promote economic relations. After several abortive efforts to get a Colorado affiliate established, a real estate company executive and civic leader named Robert Hackstaff undertook this endeavor. Hackstaff had never been to Japan and knew little of Asia but believed firmly that understanding between Americans and Japanese was important and wanted to do something to promote it. Many of Colorado's important business firms are members of the Japan America Society, which sponsors a variety of cultural and educational activities for Americans and Japanese businessmen and their families as well as ordinary citizens. One of its projects is the annual Japan Bowl in which teams of Colorado high school and college students compete, demonstrating their knowledge of the Japanese language and culture. The winning teams receive expense-paid trips to Washington, D.C., to compete against teams from all parts of the nation.

Longmont, a city of some 65,000 and less than one hour's drive north of Denver, also has a thriving sister-city relationship. Its partner is Chino in mountainous Nagano Prefecture. Longmont's interest at first was solely commercial. The initiative was sparked by the city's leading entrepreneur, Ken Pratt, then president of the Economic Development Association of Longmont (EDAL). Pratt wanted to bring to Longmont Japan's high-tech firms looking for U.S. sites where they could set up operations. The problem was how to bring the two together. One day in 1988 the Japanese owner of a die-casting plant near Lake Suwa in Nagano Prefecture told Sadao Iwashita, Colorado's commercial representative in Tokyo, that he might be interested in opening a Colorado operation in some midsized town like Longmont. And incidentally, he said, he had heard his old friend, Mayor Bunro Harada of Chino, was looking for an American sister city. At the time Larry Green, manager of EDAL, and his guide and consultant, Bill Hosokawa, were preparing to depart for Japan to introduce Longmont to prospective investors. They were instructed to visit Chino, if it was convenient, to see what it was like.

Chino is about midway between Tokyo and Nagano, where the Winter Olympics were to be held. The Americans took the train and found a neat little town of about 50,000 not far from Lake Suwa at the foot of some heavily wooded hills. From the depot they took a cab to City Hall and found a swarm of local newspaper and television reporters waiting. The visitors were astonished to learn the media was present to cover the signing of a sister cities agreement between Chino and Longmont, which had already been outlined on a scroll with an ink-brush. Unprepared for anything quite so formal, Green signed what amounted to a statement of intent, and the story was widely publicized in the local press. Some months after Green's visit a delegation from Chino—accompanied by a fetching young lady interpreter named Yoriko Kasai—came to Longmont and was entertained at, among other events, a rodeo in which some of the Japanese participated in a contest to tie a ribbon to a fleeing cow's tail.

Eventually, six blue-chip Japanese firms made investments in Longmont. The largest was a $50 million equity investment by electronics giant Matsushita in Solbourne, a fledgling U.S. company producing computer systems. Mitsubishi signed an agreement with Sherwood Enterprises for the manufacture of home automation systems. Sumitomo agreed to collaborate with Nutronics Corporation on an automobile alternator disengagement device. Mitsui Seed began work on developing superior sugar beet seed through a company called Seedex headed by Dr. Akio Suzuki, who remained in Colorado as a permanent resident after the operation was sold to the French company Florimond Desprez. Fujitsu bought Intellistor, which developed computer disk controllers, and Izumi Shoko announced plans for a precision die-casting plant. Unfortunately, when the boom went bust, many of these investors did what smart investors do—they retrenched.

A variety of gifts from Chino to Longmont is displayed proudly in Longmont's City Hall but, as in other sister city affiliations, the greatest benefit from the sister-city tie has been the student exchange program. Some of the Chino mothers were so appreciative of the hospitality shown their children by Longmont families that, under Yoriko Kasai's leadership, they organized the Aspen Club to support further exchanges, the name Aspen having been selected because of the beauty of Colorado's fall foliage.

Colorado's sister state relationship with a Japanese province was established easily despite the circumstances. In fall 1985, Morgan Smith, executive director of the state's Department of Local Affairs, traveled to China to scout prospects for Colorado business. Before leaving, he was invited by the Los Angeles office of the Japan External Trade Office (Jetro) to spend a few days in Japan on his way back from China. Smith accepted their offer to pay for hotel expenses and arrange meetings with government and business leaders.

A political issue in Colorado at the time was a campaign to repeal the state's unitary tax, a system under which the rate of taxes levied on the income of foreign corporations doing business in the state was calculated partly on that corporation's earnings worldwide. Governor Dick Lamm vigorously opposed repealing the tax. K. C. Chiwata, then president of the Japanese Pentax Camera Company's U.S. operations, which were headquartered in Denver, was outspokenly for repeal because he felt his company was unfairly being penalized, and he had exchanged some acrimonious correspondence with the governor.

Smith's first appointment in Tokyo was a meeting with Makoto Kuroda, director-general of the Ministry of International Trade and Industry (MITI), who was known for his blunt manner. Smith had hardly been seated when Kuroda asked him why Governor Lamm was speaking out so harshly about Japan's business practices. The next day at a meeting at Keidanren (Japan Federation of Economic Organizations) their outspoken director Kazuo Nukazawa showed Smith a clipping from the *New York Times* in which Lamm had expressed strong opposition to Japanese investments in the United States. Nukazawa asked if the story was accurate and, if so, why was the governor opposed to Japanese investments in particular?

In his report to Lamm after he returned to Colorado, Smith wrote:

I explained that you are deeply committed to making Americans recognize that we are losing our competitive edge, that the quality of our products has declined, that we are weak in international marketing, and that we have lost much of the drive that had helped us create the world's economy. In prodding Americans to do better, you have referred to Japan in the sense that it is out-marketing us and that we needed to get serious and compete. I am not sure that he was convinced but I recognized then that your comments are well-known in Japan and a matter of concern to the Japanese. Accordingly, I made sure that the subject was covered in every meeting, even if my hosts didn't bring it up (which was rare).

Lamm scribbled a five-word comment on Smith's report: "All paid for by Japan."

This was the situation when I told Smith that the province of Yamagata in mountainous north-central Japan had asked me to inquire whether Colorado would be interested in establishing sister state relations.

Smith was dubious but game. "This will have to be cleared by the governor, and you know how Dick feels," he said. "But let's go see him anyway."

Lamm's surprising reply was a question. "Sure, why not?"

Yamagata, in the northern part of Japan's main island, was quite similar to Colorado. It was an agricultural area—famous for its rice, cherries, apples, and grapes—just moving into the high tech age. Like Colorado, it was mountainous and had skiing and summer resorts. Incidentally, in the late nineteenth century Isabella Byrd, the British writer, had traveled widely in the Yamagata mountains before coming to Colorado where she fell in love with the area that was to become Rocky Mountain National Park.

Some months after Lamm gave his approval, Yamagata's vice-governor, Kazuo Takahashi, stopped briefly in Denver on his way to Brazil, where a substantial number of Yamagata citizens had immigrated. He did not meet Lamm but he invited Colorado's incoming governor, Roy Romer, to come for a visit. Shortly thereafter, Romer headed a delegation of Colorado businessmen to Japan and Taiwan and from Tokyo took a day off to fly to Yamagata where a big welcome reception was held for him in the high school gymnasium. As

Romer and his party entered, the high school band played *When the Saints Come Marchin' In* and the Americans were given a standing ovation.

Romer spoke briefly and graciously and invited questions from the floor. There were the usual inquiries, in Japanese, about Colorado's people and industries and an interpreter translated Romer's responses. Presently someone stood up and asked, "In Colorado's state seal, there are the words *nil sine numine*. May I ask what that means?"

Romer looked blankly at the translator. He turned to Morgan Smith who grinned weakly and shook his head. None of the American visitors knew. Then a little, white-haired gentleman in the audience stood up. Hesitantly, he cleared his throat and said, "Excuse me, I think I can help. *Nil sine numine* is Latin and it means something like 'Nothing Without Divinity' or 'Nothing Without God.' With that he sat down. Afterward the Americans learned that the Latin scholar was a beloved local English teacher named Sato.

The Americans also learned that a popular song from the 1930s that few Americans could recall, *Moonlight on the River Colorado,* was well-known and well-loved in Japan.

The Colorado-Yamagata relationship has been rewarding if not economically profitable. Yamagata has sent young bureaucrats for two-year tours of duty in the Colorado state Office of International Trade in Denver to develop business and learn about state government. Later, with the assistance of Dr. James Terada of Front Range Community College, "sister school" relations have been established between Yamagata College and Front Range, Yamagata Agricultural College and Fort Morgan Community College, the Yamagata College of Industry and Technology and Pueblo Community College, Yonezawa Women's College and Arapahoe Community College, and Higashiyama Junior High and Kent Denver Country Day School.

Yamagata Television has Harumi Kato as its Denver correspondent. And an especially warm relationship has been established between Yamagata City and Boulder based on a common interest in environmental concerns.

On June 3, 1996, in a ceremony at the Colorado state capitol attended by several hundred citizens of Yamagata and Colorado, Governor Roy Romer and Governor Kazuo Takahashi signed a "covenant" reaffirming their friendship. It read as follows:

> The State of Colorado of the United States of America and the Prefecture of Yamagata of Japan are proud to celebrate the 10th anniversary of the signing of our original sister-state agreement. We resolve to continue to cultivate friendships, deepen mutual understanding, and learn from each other through exchanges in fields such as education, culture, the arts, youth affairs, industry and economy, and pledge to promote goodwill between both countries through such exchanges. We will strive to develop environments in which children can live in a world without fear and realize lifetimes full of culture, peace and comfort. We join together to pledge our support of these goals on this third day of June in the year of 1996.

Perhaps most rewarding in the people-to-people area is the University of Denver's Understanding America program. It was originated at the university by Dr. Peter Warren as a short course for junior executives on the fast track in major Japanese businesses. The purpose was to prepare them for assignments in the United States by teaching about what Americans think and do, and why they do what they do. When recession forced Japan's corporations to cut back spending, Dr. Warren redesigned the program to focus on cultural understanding between ordinary citizens and Terada took the idea of a grass roots people-to-people exchange to Governor Takahashi. The governor thought it was such a good idea that he appropriated government funds to help pay the tuition of worthy candidates. Fifteen Yamagata citizens—men and women, young and middle-aged—come to Denver each fall to attend the University of Denver program, live in American homes, and learn what America is all about.

chapter nineteen

THE SEARCH
FOR BUSINESS

One day in spring 1979, a young, athletically built Japanese businessman arrived in Denver. His name was Isao Kamitani and he represented Japan's giant Sumitomo Trading conglomerate. His mission was to establish an office in Denver and look for opportunities for Sumitomo in Colorado's economy, which was then riding on an energy boom. The emphasis was on oil, and Kamitani had learned something about that industry during a six-and-a-half-year assignment in Houston. Kamitani's first chore was to lease an office. So many firms were coming to Denver that it took him three months to find suitable space.

Sumitomo was not the first Japanese business to discover Colorado. Kamitani found trading companies like Idemitsu had preceded him and Pentax Camera's national headquarters were in Denver. Japan Air Lines had opened a sales office here. And Kamitani had hardly settled in when other Japanese blue-chip traders—Mitsui, Nissho Iwai, Mitsubishi, Kanematsu, Marubeni, C. Itoh, Tomen—arrived to sell oil field casing and other steel items and buy everything from coal to beef.

When the boom ended less than a decade later, most Japanese traders left. Kamitani persuaded his bosses to let him stay because he was confident Sumitomo could find a place in the Colorado market-place. To begin with, he had made friends and customers of firms like Davis Oil, Anschutz, Amoco, and Chevron by providing quick deliv-ery of supplies—oil well casing, tubing, and pipe—from distribution centers he built in Casper, the Williston Basin in North Dakota, and Grand Junction.

But it took years of trying before he established a solid relation-ship with Coors. One day in Golden Kamitani saw huge Coors ware-houses full of coils of sheet aluminum waiting to be inspected before they were converted into beer cans. The warehoused aluminum was tying up capital and space. "I can save you money," he told the Coors people. "What you're doing is recycling used beverage cans. That's fine, but the way you're doing it is costing you a lot of money. I propose that you convert the recycled cans into aluminum ingots and ship the ingots to Japan. There we will roll them into aluminum sheet which will be coiled and shipped back to the port of Long Beach. I can guarantee to deliver anywhere from 700 to 1,000 tons of top quality aluminum sheet a month to Golden, as specified by Coors, on three to five days notice so you won't have the storage problem."

Coors executives laughed. They asked how he could control the quality and timing of shipments all the way from Japan. Kamitani explained Japan had perfected a system for "just in time" delivery of materials because of lack of warehouse space and to save interest on the funds tied up in inventory. Coors executives agreed to try Sumitomo's system and were astonished it worked without a hitch.

Its success led naturally to introducing Coors beer to Japan. But the introduction almost was a disaster because the demand had been underestimated. Kamitani solved the problem by a spectacular but costly promotion. He chartered the Flying Tigers' then-new Boeing 747 freighters to fly Coors beer from Stapleton International Airport to Tokyo with a refueling stop in Anchorage. In all, twenty-five planeloads of Coors beer were flown to Japanese consumers who were notified of the beer's arrival with a heavy advertising campaign that said, "Sorry to have kept you waiting; a Jumbo Jet load of Coors beer has just arrived from Colorado. Enjoy."

Japan continues to buy hundreds of millions of dollars' worth of Colorado products ranging from beef to coal to electronic goods, and ranks third behind Canada and Mexico as an export market. In 1986 the semi-official Japan External Trade Organization (JETRO) opened an office in Denver, with the personable Fumiaki Kuraishi in charge, to expedite two-way trade. He and his family lost no time in becoming part of the Denver community. His wife Yasuko, a quilting enthusiast, quickly was adopted into quilting circles. Their daughter, Makiko, graduated from Colorado College with honors, and their son, Heisuke, was chosen to play a classical piano piece at his high school graduation.

Japanese interests also invested in the booming Colorado real estate market. The Suzuki family, with extensive holdings in downtown Tokyo, purchased several office buildings now managed by one of their sons, Takayuki. The Kensuke Nakagawa family, also with property interests in Tokyo, bought a major office building but faced personal tragedy. Their younger son, Masayuki, who was enrolled at the University of Colorado in Boulder, was killed in an automobile accident in 1987. The university set aside a small plot on the campus for a Japanese-style garden in the student's memory. A plaque reads:

This garden is dedicated to the memory of Masayuki Nakagawa of Kawasaki, Japan. While enrolled on this campus he died in an auto accident with his friend Hiroshi Tadokoro. This garden was funded by a gift from the Nakagawa family in appreciation for the kindness extended by the University family. The Nakagawas hope that the garden will be a lasting symbol of friendship and understanding between the United States and Japan, a cause to which Masayuki meant to devote his life.

Masayuki Nakagawa

Feb. 6, 1953–Jan. 13, 1977

Soon after Japanese businessmen began to arrive, Kamitani and Ken Ota, the Japan Airlines representative, founded the Japan Firms Association. It was both a social and professional group to help Japanese businessmen and their families adjust to life in Colorado. One major problem they addressed was the Japanese education of the children, most of whom were grade school age. How would these youngsters catch up with their peers when their families were rotated back to Japan in a few years? The solution was a Japanese language school held Saturdays in classrooms rented from Arapahoe Community College in Littleton. One of their social highlights is the traditional Japanese spring *undokai,* a family picnic with all kinds of footraces and other competitions.

As the bloom fell from the energy boom, Japanese trading companies closed their Denver offices, one by one, until Sumitomo was the only one left. Kamitani was the last to leave, moving his office in 2003 to southern California to take care of a special project. In 2005 he retired from Sumitomo and joined the Denver law firm of Rothgerber, Johnson and Lyons as General Manager, International Business Solutions, to serve foreign clients looking to do business in the United States.

But business was not the only interest of Japanese investors. An ambitious educational opportunity involving Japan came Denver's way when the venerable Loretto Heights College, operated by an order of Catholic nuns, ran into financial difficulty. The school was closed and its spacious and handsome campus in southwest Denver was put up for sale. The sisters found a buyer in an unusual Japanese physician and educator named Dr. Shoichi Okinaga. Starting in 1959, shortly after he passed the Japanese national examination for physicians, he set out to revolutionize his country's traditional system of higher education. Before long he had founded a chain of six colleges in medicine, pharmaceutical sciences, law, liberal arts, economics, and science and engineering with a total of more than 15,000 students. Soon he expanded with affiliated schools in various parts of Japan and started a program of sending promising graduates abroad to study in noted universities like Oxford and Harvard. In the United States he made arrangements with the University of Salem in West Virginia and Marycrest University in Davenport, Iowa. He also set up Teikyo Post University in Connecticut. Then he came to Denver to announce he was buying Loretto Heights University and establishing Teikyo Loretto Heights University where Americans and students from Japan would study together in English with emphasis on intercultural and world economic and political issues.

The announcement was received with great enthusiasm in Denver. Not only would the Loretto campus be put to use again, but also Denver would become an international center with hundreds of Japanese students coming to study and, hopefully, would remember Colorado with great fondness when they returned home with U.S. degrees.

Unfortunately, that was not to be. Dr. Terada, who for a period served as president of the new college, remembers the premonition of problems he had when he met some members of the first Japanese class at the Denver airport.

"Here was this kid from Japan," he recalls, "with two golf bags over his shoulders. Where was his laptop computer? Had he come to study or to have a good time?"

What had been overlooked in the enthusiasm of getting a Japanese university in Denver was that the Japanese put great stock in degrees from prestigious schools—institutions the equivalent of Ivy League universities in the United States. The best students compete, sometimes desperately, to get into them. Teikyo Loretto did not have this status and despite its attractions it had little success in recruiting the best. One objective had been to enroll Americans in Teikyo Loretto to create a good cultural mix on campus. But the university was successful in becoming accredited only to the Accrediting Council for Independent Colleges and Schools, under which it was not qualified to award doctorates. Therefore, it was not particularly attractive to serious American students despite the opportunity to get to know young Japanese. Although the campus originally was designed to accommodate as many as 1,600 students, its enrollment has been around 150 Japanese.

chapter   twenty

CONSULAR CONNECTION

One day in 1974 Nobuhiko Ushiba, the Japanese ambassador in Washington, D.C., passed through Denver and invited me to lunch. We chatted about many things and I was under the impression the ambassador was simply trying to learn more about Colorado.

Some weeks later an official from the Japanese consulate in San Francisco called on me in Denver. After exchanging pleasantries, the official abruptly said something like: "I have the honor to inform you that my government would be honored if you would serve as our honorary consul general in Colorado."

I was caught completely off guard. The first questions that came to mind were what is a honorary consul general and what does he do? There were other questions. Would accepting a post with a foreign government affect my U.S. citizenship? How much time would the position require? How would my employer feel about this?

I thanked my visitor and asked for time to think about the invitation. I talked with my wife, Alice, and thought deeply about my relations with Japan. Yes, I was of Japanese ancestry and had more than a passing interest in Japan. But then again it was Japan that had attacked my country and launched the war that landed me in an American prison camp. I wanted the United States and Japan to get along, but could I accept an honorary position to serve Japan without compromising my position as an American?

The next day I talked to my boss, Palmer Hoyt, who had no objection to his employee accepting the post if it did not take too much time and there was no conflict of interest. In fact, the boss said, the appointment would be quite an honor for both the employee and the paper. Great, but one couldn't be too careful. To cover all bases I talked to the U.S. attorney and the head of the FBI office in Colorado. They saw no problem. "Japan is our friend and ally now," one of them said. Finally I talked to my friend Benjamin Stapleton, an attorney, honorary consul of France, and dean of the Consular Corps of Colorado. Stapleton explained the Consular Corps had several dozen members, virtually all of whom were Denverites serving as honorary consuls or consuls general for a foreign country with which they had an ethnic or business tie, or in some cases no tie at all. For example, Dwight Hamilton, also an attorney, was honorary consul of Korea with which he had no connection other than having served there with the U.S. Army during the Korean War. "We'd be delighted to have Japan represented," Stapleton said.

So I accepted the invitation and was named honorary consul general of Japan in Colorado, someone Japanese nationals could go to locally if they encountered problems having to do with their nationality.

Consular offices have a variety of functions. For example, an American living abroad for any length of time would register at the nearest U.S. consular office to make his presence known and to seek assistance if it should be required. Japanese nationals—as distinguished from Nisei who are U.S. citizens—in Colorado registered at the consulate general in San Francisco whose territory included the northern half of California, Nevada, Utah, and Colorado. Of course the consular office was closed during the war but when diplomatic relations were restored, a Japanese official from San Francisco visited Denver periodically to see how his people were doing, catch up on the latest news, and take care of such routine chores as renewing passports.

Passport renewal was especially important. The regulations allowed a Japanese national to apply for renewal by mail, but he was required to pick up the renewed passport in person. For a Denver resident, it meant flying to San Francisco, taking a bus or cab to the consulate, claiming the passport, and possibly having to remain overnight before flying back to Denver. Aside from the expense, such trips required time away from work that many applicants could ill afford. And because a consular official would come to Denver only every six months or so, many individuals were inconvenienced. Thus, with my appointment as an honorary consul, Japanese nationals began to show up frequently at the *Denver Post* to claim their renewed passports.

The consular official was also responsible for learning about possible candidates for a decoration from the emperor, an exceedingly high honor granted in recognition of extraordinarily meritorious service and contributions to Japan and Japanese-American relations. Ordinary Japanese in the home country could not even dream of such an honor; a Japanese immigrant who had sprung from humble beginnings could only fantasize about it.

There were four orders of awards. The first, called Supreme Order of the Chrysanthemum, was reserved for presentation to foreign heads of state. This was followed by the Order of the Rising Sun (Kyoku Jitsu Sho), which had eight grades or levels of importance with the first grade being the most important, the Order of the Sacred Treasure (Zui Ho Sho), which itself had six grades, and the Order of the Precious Crown (Hokan Sho), which was reserved for women and had eight grades.

The first Colorado Japanese to receive a decoration was Dr. Konai Miyamoto, who in 1957 was awarded the Order of the Sacred Treasure, Fifth Grade, and it was presented to him with great ceremony. Eight years later, in 1965, Seishiro Nakamura, a pioneer farmer and community leader, also received the Order of the Sacred Treasure, Fifth Grade. In 1966 Dr. Eizo Hayano was recipient of the same decoration.

Two years later, in 1968, Rev. Hisanori Kano was awarded the Order of the Sacred Treasure, Fourth Grade. That same year three other Colorado Issei received the Order of the Sacred Treasure, Fifth Grade: Yutaka Inai, Shigeroman Suehiro, and Kikutaro Mayeda. Honorees since 1968 are the following:

1970: Masakuni Iguchi, Order of the Sacred Treasure, Fifth Grade

1971: Mrs. Takino Takamatsu, Order of the Sacred Treasure, Fifth Grade

Mrs. Yuri Noda, Order of the Sacred Treasure, Sixth Grade

1972: Takeshi Nakamura, Order of the Sacred Treasure, Fifth Grade

Matajiro Watada, Order of the Sacred Treasure, Fifth Grade

1973: Eijiro Kawamura, Order of the Sacred Treasure, Fifth Grade

1974: Rev. Yoshitaka Tamai, Order of the Sacred Treasure, Fourth Grade

1975: Ikuji Kumagai, Order of the Sacred Treasure, Sixth Grade

1976: Genta Nakamura, Order of the Sacred Treasure, Fifth Grade

1978: Yuzo Honda, Order of the Sacred Treasure, Sixth Grade

1983: Kuichi Inouye, Order of the Rising Sun, Sixth Grade

1984: Yasuna Frank Torizawa, Order of the Sacred Treasure, Sixth Grade

1986: Mrs. Sadako Tsubokawa, Order of the Sacred Treasure, Fifth Grade

The first U.S. citizen in Colorado to be decorated by Japan was Mrs. Elizabeth Rose, who was awarded the Order of the Precious Crown, Butterfly (Third Grade) in 1977 in recognition of her work, among other activities, in helping to establish the United Nations University in Japan. Mrs. Rose was also among the founders of the Denver-Takayama Sister Cities program.

In 1982 Winfield P. Niblo of Denver was awarded the Order of the Sacred Treasure (Third Grade). He was among the first U.S. civilians to enter Nagasaki after the surrender. In an effort to break down the barriers that existed between Japanese men and women teachers, he started square dancing classes, a movement that spread throughout Japan. (One of Niblo's treasured mementoes is a letter from Prince Takihito Mikasa, which recalls that "Sapporo is the place which I was first taught the square dance by you and I recall with full of my heart on that time.") After his experience in Japan Niblo made a career of helping people through the Asia Foundation's relief programs.

Other U.S. citizens in Colorado who have been decorated are the following:

1987: William K. Hosokawa, Order of the Rising Sun, Third Grade, Gold Rays with Neck Ribbon

1988: James Tsutomu Kanemoto, Order of the Rising Sun, Fifth Grade, Gold and Silver Rays

1988: Dr. Willie Tsunetake Nagai, Order of the Sacred Treasure, Fourth Grade, Gold Rays with Rosette

2000: Robert Yoshiharu Sakata, Order of the Sacred Treasure, Fourth Grade, Gold Rays with Rosette

2001: Dr. James Hiroshi Terada, Order of the Rising Sun, Fifth Grade, Gold and Silver Rays

2005: Martin Fredman, CEO of Colorado Ballet, Order of the Rising Sun, Fourth Grade

Late in 1998 the Japanese Foreign Ministry announced it was opening a fulltime consulate general in Denver with its jurisdiction to include Utah, Wyoming, New Mexico, and Colorado. A task force came to Denver from the consular office in San Francisco to lease and equip suitable downtown office space, hire a local staff, and purchase or lease an appropriate official residence for the consul general. No ordinary house would do. It had to be appropriate for entertaining at intimate dinners or cocktail parties for a hundred or more.

Denver at the time was in the middle of a real state boom and prices for larger homes had soared higher than the Foreign Ministry was prepared to pay. The solution was found in the person of Kimihito Kamori, a Japanese investor and former Denver resident who had owned the Steamboat Springs ski resort. It was arranged that Kamori would buy a home chosen by the Foreign Ministry and then lease it to the consulate general. The building they chose was a mansion with a swimming pool not far from the Cherry Hills Country Club.

Its first occupant was Consul General Makoto Mizutani, whose previous position was minister in the Japanese embassy in Brazil. Mizutani was an outgoing individual with a good command of English and made friends quickly. He found the official residence needed some minor repairs and received approval for the expenditures from Tokyo. When the repairs cost less than expected, he used the surplus to purchase some furniture and a large painting to add warmth to the main reception room.

This was a mistake. In his effort to get the consulate functioning as quickly as possible he had failed to clear this with the money-counters in Tokyo who were in the midst of a sensational investigation of alleged misuse of funds in another embassy. The Tokyo press lost no time in jumping on the Denver story. The word "embezzlement" appeared in headlines, implying Mizutani was scheming to take with him as personal property, after his tour of duty, the furniture and artwork bought with government funds. Ultimately, the government dropped all charges, but Mizutani resigned from the Foreign Ministry. It was a loss to his country. He had been one of Japan's few Middle East specialists, having spent seven years on assignment in Egypt, Lebanon, and Saudi Arabia, during which he gained competence in both spoken and written Arabic. Indeed, one of his books was a translation from Arabic to Japanese of the autobiography of a renowned Muslim philosopher.

Mizutani's successor in Denver was Koichiro Seki who had been with Japan's mission to the United Nations in New York. Seki's overseas assignments had been in places like Hong Kong and Norway and his specialty was international law covering fisheries. After two and a half years in Denver, he was reassigned to Tokyo in March 2004.

His successor was Yuzo Ota who previously had served as minister in the Japanese embassy in New Zealand. He also had served in a similar capacity in Tanzania, as first secretary in Bangladesh, as consul in New York, and as deputy consul general in Los Angeles. He entered the Foreign Ministry in 1974 after graduation from Tokyo University and also attended Duke and Northwestern University in the United States.

chapter twenty-one

SUSHI EVERYONE?

The most recent Yellow Pages of the Denver-area telephone directory list forty-six Japanese restaurants and the names of twenty-one of them include the word "sushi." "Akebono Seafood and Sushi Bar" is at the head of the list and, next to last, is "Yoshi Tei Japanese Restaurant & Sushi."

But that is only a part of the story of changing American tastes. There is hardly a ski town in the Colorado Rockies without a sushi restaurant or two catering to trendy Americans. You can't have good sushi without fresh fish and in the last decade several wholesalers have set up new lines of business in the Denver area to supply this need. The largest is True World Foods, part of a national chain of nineteen fish wholesalers with headquarters in New Jersey. The Denver manager, Sang K. Yuh Yoshimoto, opened his outlet in 1998 with 30 regular customers. Seven years later, Yoshimoto says, he supplies fresh fish to some 120 sushi restaurants, but only one-third of them are Japanese. Most of the others are operated by Koreans and Vietnamese.

In recent years sushi, if not yet as common as spaghetti, seems to be closing in on pizza and tacos as a significant part of the non-indigenous diet of hip young Americans. There are many varieties of sushi and most of them feature uncooked fish. The most familiar form of sushi is rice lightly flavored with vinegar and delicately molded by the sushi chef into a lump about the size and shape of a Baby Ruth chocolate bar. The sushi chef then tops the rice with a slice of exceed-ingly fresh, uncooked saltwater fish, such as tuna, albacore, sea bass, salmon, or lightly boiled shrimp or octopus. Americans have learned the delicate art of dipping the sushi, fish-side down, in a little soy sauce spiked with fiery green wasabi horseradish, then consuming it in one or two quick bites.

The delicate flavor and texture of the freshest fish, which is too fresh to smell fishy, is the appeal of the sushi that Americans have come to know. Wholesalers like True World Foods scout the far reaches of the world for the freshest and best. The giant bluefin tuna, which may weigh as much as 600 pounds and command bids as high as $15,000 at auctions, are flown to Denver from Boston. Miami, San Diego, San Francisco, and Seattle, as well as Chile, New Zealand, Norway, Japan, and Africa are other sources for mackerel, salmon, sea bass, octopus, giant clams, crab, and shrimp in a variety of sizes and colors. Yoshimoto's employees pick up fish shipments at Denver International Airport before dawn and rush back to the store where it is laid out and processed for restaurant buyers.

Oddly enough, even among Japanese Americans the now popu-lar type of sushi is largely a postwar phenomenon. This is because their roots are in old rural Japan where refrigeration—and, therefore, fresh fish—was little known. They grew up with country-style sushi called *makijushi,* vinegar-flavored rice rolled up like a jellyroll inside a sheet of dried seaweed together with additional ingredients like canned eel, boiled spinach, and other vegetables. There was also *barasushi,* which was flavored rice scrambled loosely together with the ingredients named above. And sometimes the makings of *barasushi* would be stuffed in a pouch slit into a slab of deep-fried tofu, which would be eaten like a taco. The Nisei kids called them "gunny-sacks."

It is impossible to say who introduced the kind of sushi popular in the United States today. It might have been members of the U.S. Occupation Forces in postwar Japan who tried sushi—hesitantly, no doubt—at a Japanese-sponsored banquet or drinking bout and found it tasty. Soon there were sushi chefs coming over from Japan to show Americans that raw fish was interesting and delicious eating.

Meanwhile, the Japanese popularized a fast-food dish called *gyu-don, gyu* meaning "beef" and *don* coming from the traditional *tendon,* which is a large bowl of rice topped by deep-fried shrimp and doused with a thick sauce. In *gyu-don* thinly sliced beef tenderloin is grilled very quickly and draped over the rice together with sauce. In fact, one of the first postwar Japanese enterprises in Denver was a *gyu-don* fast food restaurant called the Japanese Kitchen, which opened on Denver's Sixteenth Street, across from the now defunct May Company department store and soon enjoyed a booming lunch business.

Long before that the Japanese had discovered the gustatory delights of American beef in *sukiyaki.* Then they came up with a wonderful variation: fast-grilling thin slices of tenderloin on a lightly oiled steel sheet right in front of the customers—with a bit of showmanship adding to the fun—and serving it with a sharp sauce. They called it *teppan-yaki, teppan* meaning "steel sheet." A flashy young Japanese entrepreneur named Rocky Aoki had started a *teppan-yaki* restaurant in New York called the Benihana and it was extremely successful. Rocky's father, Yunosuke Aoki, thought it might be a good idea to set up a *teppan-yaki* restaurant for his younger son, Shiro, and after scouting around chose Denver. This would be no ordinary restaurant. Yunosuke Aoki wanted to serve *teppan-yaki* in an exotic setting, specifically an old-time, barn-size, two-story Japanese farmhouse (where in an earlier era a farmer and all his sons and their families would live together). A few of these structures, built in a style called *gassho,* were preserved as historic treasures around Takayama, Denver's sister city. Aoki's idea was to buy and take apart one of these farmhouses, reassemble it in Denver, and give Denverites the experience of enjoying a new kind of Japanese dish in an ancient and authentic Japanese setting.

However, Yunosuke Aoki ran into Japan's historic preservation laws and could not export the kind of house he wanted. So he brought an architect and some traditional Japanese carpenters to Denver and had them build a replica of a *gassho*-style farmhouse at the edge of the new Tech Center in southeastern Denver. While all this was going on, he opened a Gassho restaurant in downtown Denver in 1972 and hired Kenny Sonoda, a Tokyo native who had been in New York for several years, to come to Denver to manage the new enterprise.

Eventually Sonoda left to start his own restaurant and now operates four booming Sonoda's sushi restaurants, and the Gassho in the Tech Center is doing very well, although the Japanese chefs largely have been replaced by other ethnicities, mostly Spanish-speaking.

Meanwhile, other enterprising Japanese were jumping into the restaurant business in Denver, starting as chefs and soon going off on their own to take advantage of the booming interest in Japanese food. These enterprises range from public-spirited Mario Torito's four popular Kokoro fast-food outlets with limited menus but quick service, to genteel establishments where the dining and service are designed to be elegant and leisurely. And the variety ranges from Yoko's homey country-style place in Sakura Square run by Yoko and George Nagai, to Sushi Den, an amazing success story, to Namiko's, which has won a place in middle-class suburban Arvada.

They all have their different operating styles. Sonoda is gregarious and bouncy. (His motto is "The Best Raw Deal in Town.") Yoko Nagai seldom leaves the kitchen at Yoko's but her American-born husband George, who is the "outside man," is delighted to chat about sports or anything else. Totally unlike either is Domo, which features unusual Japanese country-style decor and menu and is operated in conjunction with an aikido school. And if you're thinking of throwing a catered sushi-on-the-spot garden party for a couple of hundred guests, Mikio Hashimoto's Japon is the place to call. During baseball season he and his sushi chefs are at Coors Field successfully competing for business with the hotdog vendors.

Not many of Sushi Den's customers would recognize the boss and chief sushi-maker, Toshihiro (Toshi-san) Kizaki, whose style is to turn out sushi and keep a low profile. He traveled a winding road with many detours on his way to running the lively, popular sushi restaurant on once mouldering South Pearl Street.

Toshi was a farm boy who grew up in western Japan with a hankering to become a sushi chef. At age nineteen he left for Tokyo and became an apprentice in a sushi shop. Although shaping sushi looks simple, it took him five years to qualify as master sushi-maker, but then he wanted to learn French cooking. Toshi's brother, Yasuhiro, older by two years, was in England learning English while working in a home for spastic children and Toshi decided to visit him before going on to Paris.

Toshi Kizaki of Sushi Den. He was chosen to prepare sushi for the emperor and empress of Japan.

But his stay in London was brief, to say the least. The airline had made the serious mistake of flying Toshi to London without a proper visa. Despite his protests in barely intelligible English, he spent only one night in England—in a holding cell—before being sent back to Tokyo. Out of funds he worked at odd jobs, including some time with a crew laying rails for a subway line, until he had enough money to go abroad again. This time he chose the United States and obtained a student visa. He did indeed enroll in English classes in Los Angeles but soon his money ran out. The Japanese manager of a sushi bar in a Best Western hotel offered to help him get a work visa if Toshi would join the staff. Toshi jumped at the chance. After three years he was thinking of going home to Japan when he met Nobuko Schwab, who had come to Los Angeles in search of a sushi chef for her new Japanese restaurant in Denver with the decidedly un-Japanese name *L'Auberge Zen,* which she and her partner, Kazuko Johnson, were running. He worked for her for six months before deciding it was time to strike out on his own.

In mid-1985 on a rundown stretch of South Pearl Street fifteen minutes from downtown Denver, Toshi found an empty site that had housed a pizzeria. He leased it and set out to convert it into a sushi restaurant with help from some local sushi-lovers he had cultivated. Unfortunately a series of not unexpected contractor snafus caused city inspections to be put off and threatened to delay the grand opening, which had been planned for the week of Christmas and New Year's.

Toshi knew that if he missed the holiday business it would be a long time before he could pay his contractors and suppliers. Fortunately the inspectors' final approval notices were tacked on the walls on December 24. Toshi hurried to the Pacific Mercantile Market to grab whatever supplies were available and got on the phone to tell friends to come down for the grand opening.

In a few years he was doing well enough to buy the whole building. To assure a dependable supply of fish fresh out of Japan's seas, he launched a Sushi Den restaurant in Fukuoka, near his home village. This location had access to the best of the day's catch and could air-freight some to Denver without delay. This may be the first instance of a Japanese restaurant founded in the United States setting up a branch in Japan. Incidentally, the Den in Sushi Den stands for "Denver."

Sushi Den was paid the ultimate compliment when it was asked to provide sushi lunches for the emperor and empress of Japan when they visited Colorado in 1996. This was an assignment with dire consequences if Toshi failed to deliver absolutely superb meals. He prepared three sets of sushi, put one away under refrigeration and delivered the other two to Longmont where the imperial couple was staying. Then he hurried back to Denver and at the time when he thought the emperor and empress were having their meal he ate the third lunch just to make sure nothing had gone wrong.

The abundance of Japanese-type restaurants in the Denver area does not seem to have discouraged new endeavors. Late in 2003 Tokyo-born but U.S.-raised Jun Makino opened the French-Japanese Junz restaurant in Parker, once a sleepy country town that has become a fashionable upscale bedroom community for Denver. In 2004 the *Rocky Mountain News* gave kudos to Junz for a sushi and miso soup appetizer followed by broiled Chilean sea bass with risotto and lobster bouillabaisse sauce. Yum.

chapter twenty-two

THE IMPERIALS

It is not easy to confirm this but Denver may be the only inland U.S. city visited on different occasions by three members of the Japanese imperial family.

Prince Hitachi, the emperor's younger brother, and his princess, Hanako, dropped in on Denver for several days in fall 1981. They were followed in 1985 by Crown Prince Hiro, who was on his way home after several years of study at Cambridge University in England. Then in early summer 1994 Emperor Akihito and Empress Michiko came to Colorado for three days in the course of a twenty-day trip that included stops in San Francisco, Washington, D.C., New York, St. Louis, Denver, and Los Angeles before heading for home by way of Honolulu. Compared to the receptions they received elsewhere, the imperial couple's Colorado visit, while warm, was also low-key and relaxing, which is the way their aides had planned the trip. In Washington, D.C., they were received by President Clinton with great pomp and ceremony at the White House. In Colorado they watched tractors chewing up the dirt on a corn and onion farm and went to the mountains hoping to see bighorn sheep, which didn't bother to show up for the royal visitors. The one thing done by all three royal parties was a visit to Bob and Joanna Sakata's farm in Brighton.

Prince Hitachi and Princess Hanako, who came to Denver in September 1981, stayed in a suite at the Hyatt Regency in downtown Denver. They called on Governor Lamm—Princess Hanako knew all about the statehouse step that is exactly one mile above sea level—and planted a tree at the Botanic Gardens before briefly visiting Sakura Square. At the Sakata home they had lunch—featuring Sakata corn on the cob—with a few prominent locals before a short tour of the fields. One day they were driven to Rocky Mountain National Park for a picnic lunch prepared by Kazuko Johnson's Kyoto restaurant. Afterward, the party drove up Trail Ridge Road to the Alpine Visitor Center at 11,796 feet (Mount Fuji is 12,388 feet tall) and rubbed elbows with throngs of tourists none of whom had any idea who the Japanese visitors were.

Prince Hiro's visit, in late summer 1985, was somewhat more eventful. Corn season was over but Bob Sakata had left several rows unharvested. The prince climbed aboard a massive tractor and held the controls while it lurched forward, grumbling loudly while it swallowed cornstalks and spit out a stream of ripe ears. After visiting Rocky Mountain National Park, the prince, wearing a cowboy hat he had received as a gift, had a buffet dinner at the University of Colorado with a number of students from Japan. As a memento the university gave the Prince a CU football helmet, which was about a dozen sizes too large.

The highlight of the prince's visit was an informal dinner for his traveling party and a few Denverites at the Palace Arms of the Brown Palace Hotel. This next point is a matter of dispute. One version is that a member of the prince's party asked one of the locals to invite Bob Sakata's attractive and unmarried young daughter, Lani, to the dinner to brighten things up a bit. Another version is that the prince, having met Lani at the Sakata farm, suggested that she be invited. In any event Lani's mother gave her permission, and Lani did attend, and one of the locals escorted her home immediately after the meal.

Preparations for the emperor's visit to Denver began long before it was announced that he and the empress were coming to the United States. A three-day, two-night stay was planned and so housing had to be arranged. A location not in downtown Denver was sought, perhaps in a quiet place like Boulder, which would be convenient for a planned visit to Rocky Mountain National Park. But no hotel in Boulder was suitable. Someone suggested the possibility of using a private home, even though the imperial couple had never stayed in a private residence on their several previous trips abroad.

One evening I happened to meet my friends, Ken and Susan Pratt, wealthy real estate developers in Longmont. "I have an odd question," I said. "Would you be willing to give up your home for a few days so a very important Japanese couple could stay there?"

The Pratts looked at each other for a moment, wondering what this was all about, and then Ken said, "Well, sure, why not?"

The Pratts lived in a large, comfortable, but not overly pretentious one-story home on about an acre of wooded, fenced-in land on a quiet street not far from downtown Longmont. An advance party from the Consulate General in San Francisco examined several other homes in Boulder and Denver's northern suburbs, but they always came back to the Pratt residence. Presently some federal security agents came to look over the area and they asked Ken Pratt to remove the hunting rifles and shotguns in a basement display case. Only then did the Pratts learn that their proposed guests were the emperor and empress of Japan. Susan Pratt did what any housewife might do in preparation for special guests: she bought new sheets for the oversized bed in the master bedroom.

The emperor's plane, a white Boeing 747, landed some distance away from the terminal at Stapleton International Airport before noon on Saturday, June 18, 1994. It had been showering sporadically that morning but the rain had stopped by the time the plane landed. The visitors, smiling and bowing graciously, were serenaded by the Colorado Children's Chorale singing the beloved *Moonlight on the River Colorado* in both English and Japanese. (Karen Gerwitz of the state's International Trade Office had scurried around Denver to find the Japanese version.) The emperor and empress, obviously delighted, shook hands with each of the singers, then they were whisked away in a nine-car caravan to a barren field on the Sakata farm west of Brighton where a large tent and rows of folding chairs had been set up near a display of Sakata's products.

Lined up on the field were about a dozen pieces of farm equipment including a number of huge tractors. Sakata's purpose was to demonstrate how with modern mechanized equipment a stretch of bare land could be plowed, harrowed, smoothed, and made ready for planting within thirty minutes. It was an impressive display of harnessed horsepower unfamiliar to the Japanese. Afterward the emperor, who wades into a muddy paddy for a ceremonial planting of rice each spring, climbed into the cab of one of the tractors and fiddled with some levers while Sakata explained how the machine worked.

The emperor's caravan then sped to Longmont and the Pratt home. While introductions were being made, a chorus of Longmont

The emperor and empress were greeted with warmth and enthusiasm during their stay in Longmont, Colorado. Here, they are visiting with Bob Sakata in Brighton.

children sang *Sakura, Sakura,* an old, familiar Japanese song about cherry blossoms, and the imperial couple again shook hands with each of them before Ken and Susan Pratt led their guests inside. That evening Susan Pratt delivered an apple pie she had baked.

The next morning the emperor and empress had an American-style breakfast served in the Pratts' sun-room by a petite blonde teen-ager named Jill Green. After they were seated Jill noticed that the table was wobbling a bit. Folding a small piece of cardboard, she ducked beneath the table to slip it under the short leg. As she struggled with the weight of the table she looked up and found herself face to face with the emperor of Japan, who was on his hands and knees trying to help her. She was awe-struck, but the emperor seemed to think it was not only proper but great fun.

Later that morning the emperor and empress in a sedan—not a limousine—headed a caravan of Japanese newspaper and television reporters to Rocky Mountain National Park where at the first point of interest a park ranger explained the various features. Then, as the sky darkened with an unexpected shower, the visitors drove off to the Moraine Museum. The imperial couple's car had to stop some yards from the museum entrance, and now in a pelting rain the Japanese media representatives witnessed something they had not seen in Japan: The emperor held an umbrella for the empress as he hurried her under shelter.

The shower ended shortly and the imperial couple was driven deeper into the park where they stopped to stroll through a meadow. A colorful alpine flower, a wild lily rising out of the sod, caught the empress's eye, and she kneeled to admire it. And like any devoted husband, the emperor took out his camera and crouched to photograph his wife. At another stop the empress, entranced by the beauty of a small lake, ran down the slope to its shore with the press in pursuit. That evening, the imperial couple, completely relaxed, hosted a dinner for Ken and Susan Pratt and other dignitaries at the Flagstaff House restaurant on Flagstaff Mountain overlooking Boulder.

Just before a luncheon hosted by Governor Roy Romer on the third and final day of the imperial visit, the Japanese government was to host a reception for 500 members of the Japanese American community in the Grand Ballroom of the Brown Palace Hotel. "We will leave it to you Denver people to decide who will be invited," they were told.

The Japanese American population in the Denver area was something in excess of 10,000. How would you choose 500 out of that number without alienating the others?

The solution was to set an arbitrary quota for each of the community organizations—twenty invitations for the Buddhist Temple, twenty for Simpson Church, twenty for the Japanese Association,

twenty for the Japanese businessmen's organization, and so forth—
and let the various organizations wrestle with the touchy problem of
distributing them among their members.

Some of the disappointment at not being able to meet the imperial couple was eased by a totally unexpected gesture. On the morning of the big day residents of Tamai Tower were given twenty minutes' notice that the emperor and empress would visit Sakura Square
on their way to the Brown Palace. When their caravan drove up, the
square was packed and the overflow lined the second-story walkway.
In prewar Japan, the blinds were drawn in buildings on streets the
emperor would travel so that no one would commit the sacrilege of
looking down on him. In Denver, scores of elderly Japanese who had
never dreamed of being able to see royalty, waved to him from above
as he smiled and waved back.

The reception at the Brown Palace was equally informal and enthusiastic. The imperial couple entered the ballroom to applause along
a roped-off passage between rows of folding chairs. The emperor
spoke briefly and graciously and his aides tried to hurry him out, but
the crowd, Issei and Nisei alike, rushed up and surrounded him. He
seemed to enjoy the attention, something that never would have happened in Japan. Nobuo Furuiye wrote, "Following the Emperor's
short speech Their Majesties came by to ask questions and inquire
about the welfare of each person and he encouraged all to work for
peace and the good of all nations. The Emperor reiterated that we all
owe a debt of gratitude to all the pioneers who came to this strange
land and made a home for future generations. . . . Their Majesties
were so personable and down to earth, they put everyone at ease."

As the emperor and empress worked their way out of the ballroom, somebody shouted, "Is it okay to give them a Banzai?"

"Sure," said a member of the imperial party, "go ahead."

So the ballroom rang with a resounding "Tennoheika, Banzai, Banzai, Banzai." The cheering was not for the descendant of the Sun Goddess on the imperial throne, but for a thoroughly pleasant, friendly, outgoing gentleman who just happened to be the emperor of Japan.

After luncheon with civic dignitaries at the Governor's Mansion, Emperor Akihito and Empress Michiko hurried to Stapleton International Airport where they were seen off by a large crowd including, among others, Mayor Wellington Webb and Governor Roy Romer.

Several years later on a visit to Japan Susan Pratt was invited to call on the emperor and empress at the Imperial Palace in Tokyo. They spent a pleasant hour recalling one of Longmont's most memorable occasions.

chapter twenty-three

STORIED QUILTS

One day in 1995 three Nisei women in Denver went to see the Smithsonian's touring exhibit of early American quilts made up of patches that told a story of the nation's strength through diversity. The three were Carolyn Takeshita, Tomoye Kumagai, and June Mochizuki. Today they don't remember who it was, but one of them asked, "Why can't we do something like this to tell the story of our people?"

They got several of their friends together for a planning meeting at the Arvada Center. The upshot was that they went to various community organizations, told of their plans, and received donations totaling about $1,000, which was used to prepare packets of cloth and instructions. Then they went out and sold their friends on the idea of recording family histories in needlework.

That was the beginning of a project involving seventy-two Japanese American women in Colorado, each offering a vignette about her family's history in designs and pictures sewed into or painted on patches of cloth that were then mounted in groups of eight. The patches were assembled and exhibited for the first time to much acclaim at the Arvada Center. Because of a lack of suitable exhibit space, however, the quilts have not been widely seen. The present plan is to donate them to the Japanese American National Museum in Los Angeles.

Following, in the words of each woman who created the pieces that went into the display, are verbal explanations of some of the stories—unfortunately there is not space for all—depicted on cloth:

> The first triangle represents the Kawakami homeland in Okayama, Japan. The original fabric is made from a doorway banner that was given to our family by Okayama relatives. The embroidery was done by my late grandmother, Shikano Iritani . . . during the long winter days on the family farm in Littleton, Colorado. The blue handkerchief triangle represents our Sansei [third] generation symbolizing how Americanized we have become.—Shirley Kawakami Tsuchimoto, Aurora.

> The quilt piece is in honor of my mother-in-law, Yukino Mayeda. The design is the brand our farm used on the sacks and boxes of vegetables that were shipped all over the United States. Without my mother-in-law's hard work, the brand would never have existed.—Sumiya Mayeda, Carol Mayeda, Longmont.

> Like all farmers' wives, my mother worked in the fields. . . . How did she sew our dresses without a pattern? How did she make such good raised donuts without a recipe? She loves flowers and planted poppy seeds among the carrots.—Helen Kimura Goto, Denver.

> From 1933 to 1938 Miyo Ikeda Katagiri taught at the Brighton Japanese language school. . . . Many of her students served as

interpreters in the U.S. military intelligence service during World War II.—Emi Katagiri Chikuma, Brighton.

Four generations of women in our family lived and grew up in the foothills of the great Rocky Mountains. We loved the mountains and the wild flowers so I felt the Colorado columbine would depict a part of our lives.—Sumie Imatani, Henderson.

The flower symbolizes my entire life here in America. When I married Joe Nakagawa in the late 1950s I joined him on his farm. The black silk background comes from a kimono which was part of a family collection and represents a time of my life in Japan before coming to the United States.—Machiko Miyoshi Nakagawa, Greeley.

The crest belongs to my mother's family. She came to Colorado as a young woman and worked in the fields alongside her husband and raised her family. The next generation in our family also worked in the fields, but with changes in time the bonnet now sits on a tractor. There have been great changes for the third generation. We now have a teacher depicted by the schoolhouse, a researcher in a lab working with a microscope, and an office manager represented by a computer.—Tsugiko Murata, Fort Lupton.

The four symbols bordering the heart depict the opportunities and diversity shared by the women in the Shioshita family. The torii is symbolic of our roots in Japan. . . . The barn and silos represent the Shioshita family in Blanca. The telephone dial represents my mother, Tay Kondo, who left the family farm to pursue a career in business in Denver. The test tube symbolizes myself, Tay Kondo's daughter. I am a microbiologist.—Cindy Kondo, Denver.

My parents came to Colorado from Poston Relocation Camp after World War II. They had lost everything and started life anew from scratch. This is my mother, who had never done farm labor, planting celery seedlings which they had started in their greenhouse.—Margaret Sonoda Komuro.

We made this block to represent my husband Harley's family— the mountains and trees represent Colorado where the family has resided for three generations. The field, tractor and barn have always been part of our lives. The musical notes represent Dick and his wife Susan, who are both professional musicians.—Betty (B. J.) Inouye, Fort Lupton.

The next patch, by Hideko Ashida Shioshita of Blanca, Colorado, displays the symbols of seven organizations in which she has been active: Blanca Community Church, Sierra Granada School, Mt. Blanca 4-H Club, Auxiliary of the National Rural Letter Carriers Association, Disabled American Veterans Auxiliary, Gray Ladies, and Retired Senior Volunteers.

Tsuyu Hatasaka arrived in America in 1922 at age 17. This quilt block represents my childhood memories of my mother carrying my little sister on her back while she was working in the fields.— Mary Tsuyu Nishiyama, Denver.

The carp swimming upstream is symbolic of strength and the will to overcome difficulties. . . . This square was created in appreciation and respect for my mother and all the pioneering women of such enormous spirit and endurance.—Tomoye Tamura Kumagai, Denver.

This crazy quilt piece depicts all the differences and similarities of fabric, prints, and creates one whole—unity—we're all one. Within diversity of human life there is unity. In the important aspects of life there are more likenesses than differences—the universalities of human experience.—Denisse Yamashita Allaire, Longmont.

FIVE FARMERS

Five stories of Colorado Japanese American farming families are told here. From the sad story of the Tanaka family in Longmont to the outrageous story of Mike Mizokami's bureaucratic persecution. And then there is the inspiring story of Bob Sakata and his wife Joanna and the unusual story of Sam Matsuda and his brothers, Toshi and Dick. And finally is the story of Jim Kanemoto's success.

The Tanaka story begins with the arrival in America of Issokichi Tanaka (later known as Frank) in 1906 when he was seventeen years old. He moved to Brighton, Colorado, the following year, and in 1908 he began farming on fifty leased acres. He must have been a self-assured young man because that same year he became a cofounder of the Japanese Association in the Brighton and Fort Lupton areas with some 160 members. He married Kimi Fukushima, daughter of a Denver innkeeper, and they had nine children—seven boys and two daughters—before he died in 1953. Five of the seven sons—George, Dick, King, Rocky, and Bobby—served in the U.S. Army during World War II.

George Tanaka, after farming for a while, moved to Gardena, California, and managed a supermarket produce department. Another son, Tom, went to Oklahoma City and opened a produce market. King moved to Hillsborough, California, and got into the import-export business. Mary had her own flower shop and Ruth married and moved to Fort Morgan.

That left Sam, Rocky, Dick, and Bobby to work together to build the 5,400-acre Tanaka Farms south of Longmont, the largest vegetable farm in Colorado—listed by *American Vegetable Grower* magazine in 1988 as the seventh largest vegetable farm in the southwestern United States—an amazingly efficient rural factory for manufacturing fresh food out of soil, water, sunshine, and sweat. At harvest time fleets of refrigerated trucks would be lined up outside the Tanaka packing shed, waiting to load and deliver Tanaka vegetables all over the West. But ill health doomed Tanaka Farms.

First, Bob died of heart problems. Then Sam, the nominal head of the operation, also was stricken with heart problems. Rocky suffered kidney trouble and was largely incapacitated. With three of the four principals lost in short order, it became impossible for the family to supervise every detail of their hugely complex farming and marketing enterprise. In 1990 Tanaka Farms declared bankruptcy and lost their land. Today Dick is the last of the Tanakas still in the vegetable-growing business, running a modest farm south of Longmont.

Mike Mizokami's story is also sad—and outrageous—and there are some mysterious overtones of corruption and a conspiracy to ruin him involving the government. It begins on the evening of July 17,

1962, when the telephone rang in the office of his farm just outside
Blanca in Colorado's San Luis Valley.

Ernest LaBarba, one of Mike's customers, was calling from Dallas and was almost hysterical. "Mike, what are you trying to do to
me?" he shouted. When he calmed down, LaBarba explained that a
truckload of spinach from Mike's farm had been seized by agents of
the Food and Drug Administration, presumably on suspicion that it
contained some illegal pesticide, and without the spinach LaBarba
would have to shut down his distributorship.

Mike was baffled. There had never been any question about his
produce. The Mizokami family had been farming in Colorado for
some sixty years and had an excellent reputation. Fukutaro Mizokami
had been one of the first Japanese to farm in the Arkansas Valley near
Rocky Ford. He specialized in onions and did well until the bottom
of the market dropped out and he had to leave his crop in the fields.
After auctioning all he owned, Fukutaro moved his family to the San
Luis Valley near Blanca, and began sharecropping, but by the time he
died in 1944 he was farming 180 acres of his own land. Farming
hadn't appealed much to Mike, the oldest son. He went to Oklahoma
State University to learn industrial electronics and had completed
advanced studies at the Coyne School in Chicago when his father
died. Mike abandoned a promising career to go home to run the farm
with his mother, two younger brothers, and three younger sisters.
He developed markets for summer spinach, which grew well in the
cool summer nights of the San Luis Valley when other areas were
sweltering. Now that lucrative crop was being threatened by some
mysterious federal order.

Mike got on the phone and tried to find some answers. Why was
the spinach in Dallas seized? What were the feds looking for? What
instigated the seizure? If there were suspicions about something, why

wasn't the spinach checked in Blanca instead of in Dallas? And why hadn't he been notified directly?

Mike got no answers. Three days later the spinach in Dallas was released. Two weeks after that he was notified a shipment of 840 bushels of spinach he sent to Boston had been seized. While Mike desperately sought answers, the spinach was released four days later. The next day another shipment to East Hartford, Connecticut, was intercepted then released without explanation after three days.

On August 10, another of Mike's customers in Jersey City, New Jersey, called to tell him the FDA had said it found a banned pesticide called heptachlor on the spinach. Mike had never seen, used, or even heard of heptachlor.

Many questions raced through Mike's mind. Who had charged before the Food and Drug Administration that Mizokami was using a forbidden chemical? Why had the FDA jeopardized Mizokami's business by seizing his products in various parts of the country instead of coming directly to his farm in Blanca? How accurate were FDA's tests? And why was all this happening?

Meanwhile, Dr. Percy B. Polen, inventor of heptachlor, obtained a sample of spinach from the FDA to retest. About the same time Mizokami retained William Bradley & Associates, a testing laboratory, to check out frozen samples of his spinach. Shortly, both experts reported they had found no heptachlor or any other contaminant. When Dr. Polen demanded to see results of the FDA tests, he was told their findings had been in error and Mizokami received a "we regret this occurrence" letter.

By then Mizokami's market had been destroyed and his remaining crop, worth nearly a half million dollars, had to be plowed under. The huge loss had a domino effect. Profits from the spinach would have gone into planting a big winter tomato crop in Sinaloa, Mexico, but now he had no money to finance it. That year Mizokami recorded a loss of a quarter million dollars. Worse, sources of the credit that large-scale farmers like Mike depend on began to dry up.

Mike took his problem to his congressman, J. Edgar Chenoweth, who agreed to introduce a bill enabling Mizokami to seek damages from the federal government. Chenoweth also testified for Mizokami at a lengthy hearing before the House Judiciary Subcommittee. In reporting that hearing, Zeke Scher of the *Denver Post* wrote:

> Chenoweth outlined the events of 1962, emphasizing that the FDA could have quickly discovered if the Mizokamis had used heptachlor. "All they had to do was ask," he said. "This appears, Mr. Chairman, to be more than the ordinary diligent effort the FDA should follow in trying to protect the interests of the consumers of this country. There are certain conclusions you must draw from the facts. Whether it was a conspiracy or not, it was obvious it was an effort to find something in the spinach to discredit the Mizokami brothers. The FDA people did not only check one car but car after car after car looking for this heptachlor.
>
> "Apparently they (the FDA) have two or three ways of testing for heptachlor. They said they used one test and apparently there was heptachlor in the spinach but when they sent it to the Washington office they said there was none. . . . I feel the Mizokamis have suffered great injustice and great damages."

The Mizokamis' attorney, Francis Trowbridge Vom Baur, declared the action the Mizokamis sought was an effort to redress the catastrophe they had suffered through no fault of their own.

"For some very obscure reason," Vom Baur said, "during July and early August 1962, the FDA people had singled out the Mizokamis and were going after them and going after them alone. They intercepted and stopped the Mizokamis' spinach shipments in various parts of the country, while Mizokamis' competitors were unmolested. . . .

[T]he results of these tests were uniformly favorable. Nevertheless, it was perfectly clear to the customers that, for some reason the FDA was going after Mizokami spinach shipments. . . . It raised doubts in the customers' minds as to quality, safety and salability of Mizokami spinach."

On October 6, 1964, President Lyndon Johnson signed Private Law 88-346 authorizing the U.S. Court of Claims to award damages to the Mizokamis. The Court of Claims began its own investigation, which uncovered records, according to the *Denver Post,* that showed the Denver office of FDA had ordered seizure of Mizokami spinach based on "telephone conversations" with unidentified individuals who said there was heptachlor on Mizokami spinach. These sources were never identified.

Ultimately Mizokami was awarded a judgment of $353,929. He estimates his loss over six years—unable to sell crops, he was unable to keep up mortgage payments and he lost much of his land and equipment—was more than five million dollars. He had made forty-two trips to Washington, D.C., in his efforts to clear his name. Mizokami lives quietly today in Glendale, Arizona, farming on a limited scale in Mexico with his sons.

By contrast, Bob Sakata's story is heartwarmingly upbeat. It is a story of how the faith and generosity of one man started an ambitious teenager on the road that led him to positions of leadership in his profession, in his community, and in public service. It starts on a leased twenty-acre farm on the east shore of San Francisco Bay where Bob's widowed immigrant father, Mantaro, struggled to keep his family of four children together. The oldest was a son, Harry, then twin girls, and finally Bob.

Bob was fifteen years old when war came in 1941. The family was forced to abandon their home for the Topaz war relocation camp in Utah. Harry was the first to leave the camp to top sugar beets in Idaho. Bob, fretting over idleness in the camp, wrote to Jack Clevenger, his Future Farmers of America leader in junior high school who had become dean of the agriculture college at Colorado State University in Fort Collins, and asked for help in attending the school. Clevenger was able to help Bob out of the camp in late 1943 but couldn't get him into the university because Bob had not completed high school. Bob went to Brighton, a short distance north of Denver, stayed briefly with an uncle, and then struck out on his own. An elderly farmer named Bill Schluter gave Bob meals and a place to sleep in a cinder-block milk shed in return for doing some farm chores and milking a few cows while he went to high school.

One day in fall 1944 Schluter asked Bob if his family would like to own a farm in Colorado and, if so, how much money they had to buy one.

Bob thought a while and then replied, "I guess we could scrape up about $1,200. We never had much and we lost almost all of it when we were sent off to camp."

He heard no more about the matter until the following spring when Schluter sat Bob down and said something like: "Tell your folks to come out of the camp. I've just bought you a farm—40 acres with good water rights here on the outskirts of Brighton. The price is $6,000—$150 an acre—and you can pay me back whenever you can."

The land had been planted largely in sugar beets. Bob used $900 of the family's savings to buy a team of horses, a ten-year-old tractor, and other equipment needed to turn sugar beet fields into a vegetable farm. The first crop included lettuce, cabbage, tomatoes, cucumbers, onions, and green beans. Bob and his father were responsible for the field work. One innovation they introduced was chemical fertilizer instead of the barnyard manure commonly used by other farmers.

Harry bought supplies and took the produce to the Denargo whole-sale market in Denver where grocers and brokers came to stock their bins. The Sakatas astounded Schluter by repaying the loan, plus interest, after the second harvest.

Early on, Bob detected a significant trend in the vegetable market. The corner grocery stores that required only small amounts of any one vegetable were being replaced by huge supermarket chains whose buyers wanted to be assured of a steady supply of produce of uniform quality. The era of food factories in the field had arrived and Bob realized he would have to gear up his operations to succeed.

After the untimely deaths of his father and Harry, Bob found support and counsel in Frank Nakata, among the younger Issei in the Brighton community, and set out alone to expand his fields as rapidly as he could afford it. Today Bob, with his wife, Joanna, and son, Robert, as partners, owns Sakata Farms, more than 3,000 acres in the Platte River Valley around and north of Brighton. (*American Vegetable Grower* lists it as the fifteenth largest in the Southwest region.) Sakata's land is in a patchwork pattern, partly because he acquired smaller farms as they became available and partly because he scattered his holdings over a large area to minimize the danger of an entire planting being wiped out by summer hailstorms. He was particularly happy to buy farms whose owners were nearing retirement. "They were going out of business anyway," Sakata explains, "and I could assure them a comfortable income for the rest of their lives."

Without an adequate supply of water, farming is impossible in the semi-arid West. Sakata made sure the farms he bought had ample water rights. When shares in water distribution companies became available, Sakata was quick to purchase them. As his operations expanded, Sakata found himself spending more and more time at a drawing board and in his maintenance shop as he designed new machines to

Bob and Robert Sakata of Sakata Farms.

speed up soil preparation, seeding, cultivating, harvesting, and pack-ing his crops. One of his inventions is a giant machine that harvests an acre of corn in an hour, doing the work of twenty-four men hand-picking the ears. His wife, who as a bride had worked alongside her husband in the fields, took charge of the expanding office chores. Their son, with degrees in microbiology, chemistry, and psychology, became general manager.

Sakata has made time to be more than just a farmer. He has been a bank director and member of the Brighton School Board. He helped found the Brighton Community Hospital and served nine years as its president. He served two terms as president of the National Sugar Beet Growers, served as president of the National Onion Growers Association, was named one of four outstanding young American farmers by the United States Junior Chamber of Commerce, was one of five members of the Agricultural Commodity Credit Board under Presidents Ford and Nixon, and is an elder at Brighton's First Presbyterian Church.

Sakata's agricultural know-how has gone international. He has been a consultant with the Hokkaido Sugar Company and the Takii Seed Company in Japan, and the Sakata (no relation) Seed Company of Kyoto. He advised the Kubota Tractor Company on ways to adapt their machinery for the U.S. market and was a consultant to Mitsubishi Heavy Industries on development of a central pivot irrigation system and improvements on forklift trucks.

All his consulting with Japanese firms is without charge. Sakata says, "It's certainly debatable whether there is any advantage to our company in return for all the time I am spending in sharing my ideas and views on technology for improving food production, but I get a good feeling to know that I may be contributing towards the betterment of society."

One of his rewards was a Japanese decoration, the Order of the Sacred Treasure, Gold Rays with Rosette, in 2000. But equally important to him is the friendship and respect of the people who work for and with him in Brighton. An honor he cherishes especially is induction in 1999, together with Joanna, to the Colorado Agricultural Hall of Fame.

In contrast to Sakata's focus on farming, Shunso Matsuda's family have built a successful company farming and raising livestock. Almost immediately after war broke out in 1941 federal agents arrested Shunso Matsuda, an Issei from Hiroshima who had risen to farm foreman near Salinas in California's Monterey County. Like other Japanese American community leaders he had been picked up for no reason other than that he was a Japanese immigrant who had gained some prominence in the community. When all persons of Japanese ancestry were ordered out of the West, his wife, Chie, and their children left to join friends in Las Animas in Colorado's Arkansas Valley. In time, the oldest of the sons, Sam, joined the Army, studied at the Military Intelligence School, and was sent to Tokyo where he served as interpreter in the war crimes trials.

Meanwhile, when the Matsudas learned that the Great Western Sugar Company was opening a plant at Hereford, close to the Wyoming line and east of Fort Collins, they moved there to find work. By 1970 Great Western's magazine, *Through the Leaves,* reported that the three Matsuda brothers—Tosh, Sam, and Dick—in partnership with Dick Woods, owned the Buckeye Land and Livestock Company. They grew sugar beets, corn, and alfalfa; fattened some 35,000 lambs each year on their Colorado property; and operated a ranch on leased land northeast of Casper, Wyoming, where 12,000 ewes and 2,000 cattle were pastured. The story also said the Matsudas set a record for their area by delivering sixty truckloads of sugar beets in one day to the Buckeye shipping station. As this is written, Sam Matsuda is retired in Wellington and his son, Dave, farms some 700 acres in the area, custom feeding lambs and growing sorghum for dairymen.

A Nisei who decided there was a better way to make a living than farming, and succeeded eminently, is Jim Kanemoto of Longmont. He was born in 1917 to Goroku and Setsuno Kanemoto, immigrants from Hiroshima, who were farming near LaSalle, Colorado. In 1935 Jim was living in the Denver Buddhist Temple dormitory and attending Manual Training High School when his father died in an automobile accident. Jim hurried home to take over the family's eighty-acre farm on rented land just outside of Longmont. Goroku by law could not own land. But Jim, as a citizen, could, and he saw no advantage in continuing to be a renter. Shortly, he and his brother, George, younger by two years, contracted to buy 140 acres off South Main Street on what was then Longmont's southern outskirts. Eventually their holdings grew into a 350-acre vegetable farm with a retail market on South Main.

By 1944 Jim felt secure enough to marry Chiyo Miyasaki from another Colorado farming family. (And four years later George married Chiyo's sister, Jane.) "We worked hard together," Jim recalls. "Sometimes, when I was extra busy in the fields, Chiyo would help load up the truck, drive a load of vegetables to the Denargo market in Denver, sell the produce, and then buy fruits and other stuff to sell at the market we were running."

In winter, when there was time to spare, Jim tinkered with ideas for improving farming methods. One was a portable dam that could be placed in an irrigation ditch to regulate the volume of water diverted to the fields. Kanemoto patented it and in 1960 founded the Kane Manufacturing Company to manufacture and market it.

Meanwhile, Jim and George viewed with interest the rapid development of the area after IBM built a huge plant midway between Longmont and Boulder. It occurred to the brothers that it might be wiser to grow houses and commercial buildings on their land rather than vegetables.

In 1961 they annexed 350 acres to the city of Longmont, laid sewer and water lines, and put up homesites for sale in a development called Southmoor Park. Obviously a new subdivision needed schools and open space. The Kanemotos gave the city ten acres for a grade school and an administration building, land for a fire station, six acres for a park (which was named Kanemoto Park), and land for the St. Vrain River Greenway that leads through the area. They also gave land for a new church to St. Stephen's Episcopal congregation.

In 1969 Jim and Chiyo went to Japan on a tour sponsored by a Buddhist group. With them were four Longmont friends, Vernon and Marge Golden and John and Esther Schlagel. Among the sights they admired was an ancient pagoda symbolizing compassion, peace, and love. The visitors were deeply moved by its beauty, serenity, and the universality of its teachings. "Why," Jim asked himself, "can't we have something like this in Longmont?"

Back home in Longmont, Jim found an engineer from India at Colorado State University in Fort Collins who said he could design a pagoda. Gradually, a five-level pagoda, sixty feet tall, began to take shape at one edge of Kanemoto Park. It was named the Tower of Compassion and presented to the citizens of Longmont—"To express our gratitude for the opportunity given the Kanemoto families," Jim said at a ceremony in 1972 attended by Governor John Vanderhoof. A plaque at the site explains the spirit of the tower: "Compassion is to live the life of love, empathy, understanding and gratitude for all things, and giving selflessly of oneself for the happiness of all beings."

Each level of the pagoda has a meaning, which Kanemoto explains in this way:

> The first level stands for Love. If I truly love someone, I must love all humanity. How can I really love one person if I hate others?
>
> The second level stands for Empathy. Your happiness is my happiness. Your sadness is my sadness. I feel your pain and I share your joy.

The Tower of Compassion, a Buddhist pagoda presented to the city by Jimmie Kanemoto, one of Longmont's most prominent citizens.

The third level stands for Understanding. We as humans must understand each other for mankind is one. We are all interdependent. How can I alone be happy if my family is sad? How can we Americans be really happy when more than half the people of the world go to bed hungry?

The fourth level stands for Gratitude. We must have a sense of gratitude for all that has been given us. I am here because of my parents. The food I need for nourishment comes from the land. The shelter of my home comes from the trees. The knowledge that I have came from my parents, my teachers, and many others. Therefore what I am is the total sum of others. So I must have gratitude to all things.

The fifth level stands for Giving Selflessly of Oneself. As I give myself to others, strangely enough I find myself and I find true happiness.

When all these are put together, they become the essence of true compassion. This is what the Tower of Compassion stands for.

Compassion has been adopted as one of its tenets by the Longmont Rotary Club, which gives a $1,000 scholarship each year with a plaque memorializing the Tower of Compassion.

Meanwhile, Kanemoto was busy with many other community activities. He has served on the Water Board, Community Hospital Foundation, the Economic Development Association (which he represented on several state-sponsored trips to Japan), and the board of the First National Bank, and as president of the Longmont Rotary Club, and the first president of the Fox Hills Country Club, and member of the Longmont Long Range Planning Committee. Outside of Longmont he has served as president of the Buddhist Churches of America and Denver's Sakura Square project. The government of Japan decorated him in 1988 with the Order of the Rising Sun, Gold and Silver Rays.

In 1996 Kanemoto was inducted into the Boulder County Business Hall of Fame. In accepting the award he acknowledged the role Chiyo and his brother, George, and George's wife, Jane, have played in his life. "Our greatest achievement," he said, "is that our partnership has existed for sixty-one years, first my brother and I, and then with our wives. The four of us have worked together through many hard times and, by good fortune, prospered together. Our trust in each other is such that we still share one bank account. It was the support of my wife, and George and his wife, that enabled me to make my small contribution to our community."

Community service is continuing through the next generations. Jim's son, Ken, and George's son, Ed, and grandson, Keith, are with the Prudential Real Estate firm in Longmont.

Chiyo died in 1999 after a long illness. Two Buddhist services were held in her memory, one in the First Congregational Church in Longmont for her hundreds of friends there, and the second at the Buddhist Temple in Denver.

As for Jim, he has not slowed down. But he does not expect to repeat his climb to the 14,256-foot summit of Longs Peak in 1997 at age eighty. He may have been the oldest man to scale the peak. Why did he do it? "I've looked at the mountain just about every day of my life," he says. "Just wanted to see what it was like at the top."

chapter twenty-five

THE NEWCOMERS

Before the end of World War II, no Japanese had been allowed to immigrate to the United States since March 1, 1925. That was the date the Asian Exclusion Act, barring immigration from all parts of Asia—but not Europe—went into effect.

Bitter debate in Congress had preceded passage of that racist law. In hearings held by a Senate committee, V.S. McClatchy, the full-time head of the pressure group that called itself the Japanese Exclusion League of California, testified:

> Of all the races ineligible to citizenship, the Japanese are the least
> assimilable and the most dangerous to this country. . . . With
> great pride of race, they have no idea of assimilating in the sense
> of amalgamation. They do not come to this country with any
> desire or any intent to lose their racial or national identity. They
> come here specifically and professedly for the purpose of coloniz-

ing and establishing here permanently the proud Yamato race.
They never cease to be Japanese. . . . In pursuit of their intent to
colonize this country with that race they seek to secure land and
to found large families. . . . They have greater energy, greater
determination, and greater ambition than the other yellow and
brown races ineligible to citizenship, and with the same low
standard of living, hours of labor, use of women and child labor,
they naturally make more dangerous competitors in an economic
way.

Another witness, former U.S. senator James D. Phelan, told the committee, "The people of California object to the Japanese . . . because
of racial and economic reasons."

The Asian Exclusion Act was bitterly resented in Japan for its
racial discrimination, and many students of history contend that this
insult led to the rise of the militarism that led ultimately to World
War II.

But the inevitability of human nature, if not a sense of fairness,
first breached the law. Not a few American soldiers and sailors sta-
tioned in postwar Japan fell in love with and married Japanese girls.
Then they discovered their country would not permit them to bring
their brides home with them. At first members of Congress in their
home districts introduced private bills for the benefit of specific individuals. Thus a few Japanese spouses and children of U.S. servicemen
were permitted to enter the United States as exceptions to the 1924
Asian Exclusion Act. But that was a slow and laborious process, and
there were many Americans who were concerned about the racism in
the existing law.

In 1952 Congress, after intense lobbying by the Japanese American Citizens League, passed what was known as the Walter-McCarran
Immigration and Naturalization Act. It repealed the Asian Exclusion

Act of 1924 and extended to Japan and other Asian nations a token immigration quota. It also eliminated race as a bar to naturalization, a provision that was profoundly important to Issei who had spent two-thirds or more of their lives in a country that had discriminated against them as "aliens ineligible to citizenship." In communities around the United States hundreds of elderly Japanese attended classes to learn about the three branches of government—executive, legislative, and judicial—the Constitution, and other facts necessary to pass naturalization examinations. In Denver, Harry Matoba, an Issei with an American college education, tutored scores of Issei in night classes. In Brighton, John Horie coached some sixty Issei seeking naturalization. (One war bride, who will remain nameless to avoid embarrassing her, was asked by a citizenship examiner testing her loyalty whether she would be willing to fight for her new country in case of war. "No," she replied. The startled examiner asked why. "Because ladies don't fight," she said. She passed.)

The change in the law, in addition to permitting Japanese war brides to enter the United States, enabled a few members of a new generation of Japanese to move to the United States and seek citizenship. In the Japanese American communities they were called the Shin-Issei, meaning "New Issei." And in a variety of ways they have contributed to the progress and well-being, and richness of life, of America's ethnic Japanese.

Among the early arrivals in Denver was Dr. Sumiko Hennessey who founded the Asian Pacific Development Center to promote the acculturation of newcomers. War brides attended classes to learn to cope with life in America. Individuals with personal problems were counseled. Interpretation was provided for the few who had run afoul of the law. When the need for this kind of help diminished among Japanese immigrants, Dr. Hennessey's center turned its attention to the problems of a new wave of Asian immigrants from countries like Vietnam, Cambodia, Thailand, and Indonesia.

Other Japanese Americans have made a living teaching Japanese arts. Rev. Nobuko Miyake-Stoner came to the United States to attend a Methodist divinity school and became a bilingual spiritual leader both inside and outside the Japanese American community. Kyoko Kita, married to a Nisei serviceman, teaches Japanese cooking, was instrumental in founding a chapter of Ikebana International, and conducts flower arrangement classes as does Akiko Buckmaster. Miyoka Bando is a teacher of classical Japanese dancing. Junko Shigeta teaches *koto,* which is something like a horizontal harp.

Other Japanese arts have become almost commonplace. The most recent Metropolitan Denver Yellow Pages carries eighteen listings under *karaoke*—or singing with recorded accompaniment—with most of them appearing to be for rentals of tapes and playing equipment. And almost every section of the metropolitan area has *judo, karate,* and *aikido* martial arts schools.

Some members of the third (*Sansei*) generation took to *taiko,* outsized Japanese drums, in which groups of six to ten beat out stirring and thunderous rhythms. The first group, Denver Taiko, got its start in 1976 after Mark Miyoshi was introduced to *taiko* on a trip to California. Now several groups are in frequent demand for performances.

Among the newcomers were professionals, like Dr. Yuji Oishi, who served the community as a highly regarded medical photographer, and Dr. Hideya Tsuda, who is the physician at a federal correctional institution. Two Japanese women, Yoko Nagai at Yoko's and Yuri at Namiko's, own and operate their own restaurants. Seiji Tanaka, who at one time managed the Kyoto restaurant, runs an insurance agency whose clients include students at Teikyo University who are more comfortable speaking Japanese than English. Haruhisa Yamamoto and his wife manufacture tofu by the ton, and Yoshi Nakasone's M.E.M. Travel Service specializes in booking tours to Japan. Kei Izawa runs the national operations of Mont-Bell, the sports equipment firm, out of a store in Boulder and Kazunori Yamazaki is a florist.

A group of Japanese women who came to Colorado as the wives of American servicemen organized Shirakaba no Kai (Aspen Society) for mutual aid, companionship, and community service in 1989 with some 120 members. Its first president was Michie, Japanese wife of John Kanegaye, retired U.S. Air Force chief master sergeant. Many members lived in Colorado Springs, site of the Army's Fort Carson and several Air Force installations. But with passing years the membership has dwindled to less than sixty. Among their early activities was visiting elderly members of the immigrant generation to offer them an opportunity to chat in Japanese. As this is written, the Shirakaba no Kai's president is Mariko Willman of Aurora.

The publisher and editor of the *Rocky Mountain Jiho* are a Shin Issei couple, Eiichi and Yoriko Imada. The Imadas admit that the *Jiho* is not profitable and the page or two in English leave much to be desired. The *Jiho,* however, is valuable to the Japanese-reading public and without it, Colorado's Japanese American community would likely be even more fragmented than it has become by the passage of time.

A totally different publishing venture was started in 1992 by another Japanese immigrant couple, Shinsaku Sogo and his wife, Machiko. After retiring as executive director of the semi-official Japan External Trade Organization, Sogo moved to Denver and founded a nonprofit organization whose main function was producing a monthly publication called *Understanding Japan.* The monthly provided a wide range of information about contemporary Japan, presented in a lively manner to a large international audience. Unfortunately, the venture was discontinued in 2001 after Machiko Sogo's untimely death. Sogo's organization, *Sogo Way,* continues to support lectures and conferences promoting understanding between Americans and Japanese.

The experience of Kimiko Side, whose community activities are related in other chapters, is heartwarming if not entirely typical. She and her American husband, Gene, moved to Denver from Tokyo in 1959 and opened an Oriental gift shop with a $200 investment. That grew to three shops, and eventually into a wholesale business now operated by their son, Dan. With more time on her hands she threw herself into community activities, supporting the Buddhist Temple and the Methodist church, the Denver-Takayama sister city relationship, the Japanese Association, and the Japanese American Citizens League.

On her initial trip to the United States in 1955, in Miami, Florida, she was made aware of racial prejudice for the first time when she was told to move to the front of a city bus—even though she was not white—because only blacks sat in the back. Although she knew of the discrimination that Japanese faced in the United States in an earlier time, she has not experienced racial prejudice and she credits that in large part to the exemplary citizenship of Japanese Americans.

"I have spent more than half my life in America," she says. "I have three sisters in Japan, and many happy memories, but this is my country now and I wouldn't return to Japan to live for any reason. My roots have gone deep into American soil and my allegiance is to this country."

chapter twenty-six

A DAY TO REMEMBER

The following is a column written in 2003 by the author for *Pacific Citizen,* the weekly publication of the Japanese American Citizens League.

Congressman Mike Honda, the California Democrat, has introduced a resolution in the House of Representatives that would designate the 19th day of February as National Day of Remembrance. February 19 is the day President Franklin Delano Roosevelt in 1942, in a time of war hysteria, signed Executive Order 9066, which led to the imprisonment of 115,000 Japanese Americans and suspension of their civil rights without the due process guaranteed by the Constitution. Honda's proposal, press reports indicate, has substantial support in Congress.

Congressman Honda's resolution would set aside February 19 as the occasion to remember a nation's shame as it sent some of its citizens, on the basis of their race, into exile. It would be a day to contemplate the circumstances behind the callous disregard for the principles that distinguish America, an occasion to remember the tears that were shed by the victims and the desperation and heartbreak that never should have occurred. True, the nation already has done penance. President Ford went through the formality of abolishing an already invalid 9066. President Reagan signed legislation to redress—in small measure—the victims of 9066. The first Bush signed a formal apology in distributing token recompense.

But there is another side to the day of shame and infamy. February 19, 1942, marks the beginning of the end of a society in which:

♦ Nisei in Los Angeles with Phi Beta Kappa keys hidden away in their ghetto homes made a living stacking oranges in fruit markets because other doors to employment were closed to them;

♦ Nisei in San Francisco were happy to be employed for $15 a week as clerks in Grant Avenue Oriental art goods stores;

♦ Nisei from Seattle worked 60-hour weeks in summer for $35 a month, a bunk and meals mostly of rice, in Alaskan salmon canneries to help support their families;

♦ Nisei with the education and skills to be lawyers and doctors, scientists and business executives and engineers and teachers, turned to Japan for their futures because race prejudice denied them opportunities in their native land;

♦ Issei who cleared the brush and literally turned the deserts of the West into farms, orchards and vineyards were not permitted to own the land they tilled because they were stigmatized as aliens ineligible to citizenship.

Although we could not understand it at the time, relief from those racially based injustices began even as we were driven at bayonet-point into American-style concentration camps. Ironically, it was the dispersal of Japanese Americans from the camps under the government's forced "relocation" program that gave them hitherto nonexisting integration opportunities. Change was accelerated by the amazing courage of Japanese Americans who went to war in defense of the country that held their families behind barbed wire.

Today, Japanese Americans are part and parcel of their country. They, like Honda himself, serve at the highest levels of government. They, like Norman Mineta, have served in the cabinets of two presidents. They direct medical and scientific research, heal the ailing, provide spiritual counseling, administer universities, head business corporations, drill for oil and grow vast quantities of the nation's food supply, run city governments, administer justice through the courts, create beauty as artists and musicians, educate the children who are the nation's future.

Times have changed for a once reviled people. That change began even as tears flowed on the original Day of Remembrance back in 1942. February 19th is a sad anniversary, but a good day to remember, in Colorado and everywhere that good people believe in justice.

chapter twenty-seven

WHY?

You will also witness the tremendous contributions
Japanese Americans have made to our society and the
growing influence of the Japanese cultural heritage in
America. The list is long. It includes distinguished
artists and musicians. It includes business leaders and
eminent leaders of our political system.

—President Bill Clinton in his speech welcoming
Emperor Akihito to the United States on June 13, 1994

This book opened with questions from a visitor from Japan.
"What," he asked, "have the Japanese—people from my country and
their descendents—what have they done in the century they have been
in Colorado to make it a better state, a better place? What have they
done for themselves, and for America?"

The one-word answer was "much," and the chapters that followed have tried to provide the details, the "what" of their history.

But two important questions remain unanswered: How? and
Why?

How and why were these people able to rise from an impoverished background in the face of virulent race prejudice and the bitterness of war into positions not only of security and acceptance, but of
respect and leadership in this state and in this nation within a century
of time?

The answers to these questions are critical in understanding the story of a people. There probably are many explanations, and only a few of them follow. But most of the individuals questioned on this matter agreed on one point: credit the Japanese culture.

Rev. Minoru Mochizuki, a San Francisco–born Presbyterian minister retired in Denver, who has spent most of his adult life outside the Japanese American community, says, "Although we have been quite thoroughly Americanized with Western thought and philosophy, and even though many of us have become Christians, our characters and outlook have been deeply impressed by important cultural underpinnings that we have inherited and internalized from our Issei parents."

But what is the Japanese culture?

In large part it is made up of many elements—philosophical concepts or words to live by. Dr. James Taguchi, a Colorado-born physician, suggests these:

Gaman—To endure.

Gambaru—To hang tough. To persist.

Giri—Duty.

Haji—Shame, which is to be avoided at all costs. Don't shame yourselves or your families.

Oya-koko—Filial piety.

Gomen—I beg your forgiveness, a gesture of humility.

Shimbo—To persevere.

Shikata ga nai—Can't be helped. Acceptance of misfortune.

Shinsetsu—Kindness.

Dojyo—Tolerance.

Issho-kenmei—To do one's best.

Gisei—Sacrifice.

Of course many of these are moral concepts and cultural practices shared by many other civilizations. Some observers theorize that in Japan life over the centuries in a crowded land of limited resources helped to shape and sharpen traits and values that enabled the people to cope with hardship. Oddly enough, it may be said that underlying these concepts is passivity and acceptance of fate; there is little sense of triumph or aggression or glory in success. It is more important that one has done one's best—*issho-kenmei.*

Eric Saul, former curator of the U.S. Army's Presidio Museum and military historian, recognized some of these characteristics in a speech extolling the record of Japanese American soldiers in World War II. He asked why Japanese Americans had joined the Army and, in the face of discrimination and mistreatment, become "the most decorated Army unit that this country has ever produced." Then Saul provided answers: "There were words like *giri* and *ohn* which your parents taught you, which mean 'duty' and 'honor' and 'responsibility.' *Oya-koko,* love for family. You loved your families and you had to prove your loyalty at any cost. . . . *Kodomo no tame ni*—for the sake of the children. You knew you didn't want your children to have to suffer as you did. . . . *Haji.* Don't bring shame to your family. When you go off to war, fight for your country, return if you can, but die if you must."

Eiichi Imada, the newspaper publisher, recalls that Father Luis Flores, a Portuguese missionary, reached Japan in 1563 and wrote that he was impressed by the Japanese work ethic and their passion for perfection. In the United States, Imada contends, people work to live but in the Japanese tradition one works primarily for pride of accomplishment. "They are driven to excel," he says, "and they brought that trait with them."

That may be so, but it can be argued that early Japanese immigrants were more concerned about surviving than excelling at what they did. And they cooperated rather than competed with each other, because sometimes they needed help.

"Buddhist temples teach interdependence rather than individualism," Rev. Kanya Okamoto points out. "The fund-raising programs for the Buddhist Temple are all group participation. Another tradition that has carried over from Japan is the funeral *koden,* or monetary offering at funerals. *Ko* means incense. *Den* means chanting the sutra. Members of the community bring *koden* to the funeral and help pay for it, and everyone who is an active part of the community gets a proper funeral."

It may be noteworthy that Japanese American Christians also observe *koden* solatiums although incense has no part in their rites.

The sense of community was exhibited in the earlier days of immigration by an institution called *tanomoshi,* a kind of mutual savings club. A *tanomoshi* was made up of fifteen or twenty men or families who were close, with each member investing a modest and equal amount monthly into the *tanomoshi.* Members could borrow from the *tanomoshi* for any good reason—paying off bills, expanding business, making a trip to the homeland—competing with each other when there was a heavy demand for loans by bidding higher rates of interest. The *tanomoshi* were particularly useful at a time when many commercial banks were reluctant to lend to Japanese. In later years, when commercial loans became easier to get, *tanomoshi* groups became investment clubs with a large social function.

Another example of group-help is the annual Japanese American Community Graduation Program in Denver. The various groups and clubs get together to sponsor a banquet where cash awards are distributed to outstanding high school seniors to be used to pay for studies at any college, vocational or technical school. Various organizations—churches, clubs, and even individuals—provide scholarships as high as several thousand dollars. The program is administered by volunteers from among previous scholarship winners. At one time individual organizations held award functions for their own members but for the last decade the graduates' banquet has become a well-attended community affair.

Delinquency and poverty are little known in the Denver Japanese American community but Rev. Mark Heiss, pastor of the Simpson United Methodist Church, recalls that not long ago he was asked by the Denver Rescue Mission to counsel the first Japanese American ever to have come there for help. The two had a long talk, and Heiss gained some insights before he helped the youth return to his family in California. The minister says,

The rise from impoverishment, prejudice, and internment to acceptance, respect, and leadership by Japanese Americans is a singular human experience on the American cultural landscape. To be sure, there are many factors at work here. I would want to include the high expectations parents have for their children and the sacrifices parents are willing to make on their children's behalf. The American value of wanting our children's lives to be better than ours has been and is very fertile soil for Japanese American community values.

Japanese American culture teaches a strong sense of self-worth inseparably tied to a practical humility, eschewing any kind of entitlement no matter how well deserved. I think this has roots in some of the "no-self" spirituality of Buddhism, and also finds Christian support in some of Jesus's teachings such as "the first shall be last," and "the greatest is the servant of all."

This self-confident egoless-ness is a powerful and admired way of living. For me, it brings to mind the teachings of Ghandi, Mother Theresa, Jesus, and Buddha. As an outsider, these are qualities of character that I see promoted and lived out at many levels in the Japanese American community.

There are many questions that arise in trying to explain anything as complex as group character, or a minority ethic. One of them is: If Japanese virtues were so important to the development of Japanese Americans, why didn't they become Japanese instead of the 110% Americans they have been accused of being?

Mochizuki offers a plausible explanation: "We Nisei grew up within the American culture. We went to the public schools, read the daily newspapers, saw Hollywood movies. We were immersed in the American culture day after day, except at home where we came under the influence of the Japanese culture. There, our American culture was modified somewhat and fortified by Japanese values. There was no conflict, although sometimes we thought there was. The two harmonized and reinforced each other, and the result was a great combination."

And many would agree. Isn't the melding of cultures what America is all about?

Yes, and that helps to answer another question: If the Japanese part of their culture had such a large part in the shaping of their lives, would the individuals called Japanese Americans have been as "successful" if they had been born and grown up in Japan and had never been exposed to the American influence?

The author's personal, un-academic opinion: Unlikely.

It was the happy combination of the more admirable of Japanese traits being nurtured in the freedom and openness of American society that made these people what they are. Colorado was fortunate to have so many of them.

Ryozo Kato, Japan's ambassador to the United States, offered another view in a speech in late 2004 at a dinner honoring the memory of Mike Masaoka. Remembering the efforts of the Issei pioneers, Kato said,

> The Japanese term *Chi to Ase,* which literally means "blood and sweat," exemplifies how hard our ancestors had to work to overcome differences and prejudices. Even after overcoming so many hardships, it is a credit to these pioneers that they still felt the need to give something back to their new homeland. In Japanese, it is a sense of *On.*
>
> Now the next generation of Sansei, Yonsei, and even Gosei are leading the Japanese American community and creating more opportunities for closer ties between all of us. In my role as ambassador I am able to experience and monitor, on a firsthand basis, the entire U.S.-Japan relationship. I can honestly and proudly tell all of you that our relationship is the closest and best it has ever been.

SUGGESTED READING

Burton, Jeffery F., et al. *Confinement and Ethnicity: An Overview of World War II Japanese American Relocation Sites.* Tucson, AZ: Western Archeological and Conservation Center, 1999.

Chuman, Frank F. *The Bamboo People: The Law and Japanese Americans.* Del Mar, CA: Publishers, Inc., 1976.

Cohen, Morris C. "Japanese Settlement in the San Luis Valley." *The San Luis Valley Historian,* 25: 3 (1993).

Colorado Jijo Magazine. 1215 Nineteenth Street, Denver, CO 80202.

Cross, Richelle. *Pioneer Families of the South Platte Valley—Then and Now: A History of Families in the Fort Lupton Area.* Fort Lupton, CO: South Platte Valley Historical Society, 1995.

Daniels, Roger. *Concentration Camps USA: Japanese Americans and World War II.* New York, NY: Holt, Rinehart and Winston, 1972.

Final Report: The Japanese Evacuation from the West Coast. Washington, D.C.: U.S. Government Printing Office, 1942.

Hisashi, Tsurutani. *America Bound: The Japanese and Opening of the American West.* Tokyo: The Japan Times, 1989.

Honoring the Family Business: Building the American Dream, 2003. Los Angeles, CA: Japanese American National Museum, 2003.

Hosokawa, Bill. *Nisei: The Quiet Americans, Revised Edition.* Boulder: University Press of Colorado, 2002.

Ichioka, Yuji. *The Issei: The World of the First Generation Japanese Immigrants, 1885–1924.* New York, NY: The Free Press, 1988.

Inada, Lawson Fusao, ed. *Only What We Could Carry: The Japanese American Internment Experience.* Berkeley, CA: Heyday Books, 2000.

Ito, Kazuo. *Issei: A History of Japanese Immigrants in North America.* Trans. Shinichiro Nakamura and Jean S. Girard. Seattle, WA: Executive Committee for Publication of Issei, Japanese Community Service, 1973.

Japanese American Evacuation Claims Hearings. Washington, D.C.: U.S. Government Printing Office, 1954.

Levine, Ellen. *A Fence Away From Freedom.* New York, NY: G.P. Putnam's Sons, 1995.

Masaoka, Mike. *They Call Me Moses Masaoka: An American Saga.* New York, NY: William Morrow, 1987.

National Defense Migration Hearings, Part 29. San Francisco Hearings, February 21 and 23, 1942. Washington, D.C.: U.S. Government Printing Office, 1942.

Ozawa, Fumio. *Japanese American Who's Who.* Denver: Colorado Times, 1954.

Proceedings of the U.S. Circuit Court of Appeals, 10th District, in the draft evasion hearings of Robert Okamoto, Paul Nakadate, Ben Wakaya, Frank Emi, Minoru Tamesa, Sam Horino, and Guntaro Kubota, June 19, 1945.

Scher, Zeke. "The Mysterious Case of the FDA vs. Mike Mizokami." *Empire Magazine of the Denver Post* (March 13 and 20, 1969).

Spicer, Edward H., Asael T. Hansen, Katherine Luomala, and Marvin K. Opler. *Impounded People: Japanese-Americans in the Relocation Centers.* Tucson: University of Arizona Press, 1969.

The Tri-State Buddhist Church, 1916–1966. A book commemorating the 50th anniversary of the founding of the Buddhist temple. Denver, CO: Denver Buddhist Temple.

U.S. Commission on Wartime Relocation and Internment of Civilians. *Personal Justice Denied:Report of the Commission on Wartime Relocation and Internment of Civilians.* Washington, D.C.: U.S. Government Printing Office, 1982.

Weglyn, Michi. *Years of Infamy: The Untold Story of America's Concentration Camps.* William Morrow, 1976.

INDEX

Page numbers in italics indicate illustrations.

Wells, J. W., 115–16, 117, 118–19
West, C. B., 120
West Coast, 5; during World War II, 85, 87, *89, 92*
Wheat, Lori, 110
Whitfield, William H., 21
William Bradley & Associates, 223
Willis, Donald, 144
Willman, Mariko, 240
Windsor, 15
Winger, Lloyd T., 105
Woods, Dick, 230
World War II, 15; Ralph Carr's actions during, 94–96, 97–98; draft resistance during, 131–35; Issei conference during, 3–4; Japanese American concerns during, 85–87, 169; language and propaganda projects in, 137–45; military service in, 113–14, 247; newspapers during, 125–28; relocation during, 2–3, 6–7, 87–*94,* 107–12, 115–18, 225–26, 230, 242–44
WRA. *See* War Relocation Authority
Wyeno family, 96
Wyoming, 3, 32, 61, 77, 90, 132, 151; relocation center in, 7, 91, 101

Yamada, Ryoichi, 175
Yamada, Shizuo, 79
Yamagata, 183–84; cultural exchange with, 185–86
Yamagata Agricultural College, 184
Yamagata City, 185
Yamagata College of Industry and Technology, 184
Yamagata Television, 185
Yamaguchi, Frank, 15

Yamaji, Bill Iwao, 157
Yamamoto, Haruhisa, 240
Yamamoto Barber Shop, 107
Yamanouchi, Kelly, 12
Yamaoka, Ototaka, 31
Yamasaki, Kazuo, 80
Yamasaki, Yukio, 42, 64
Yamashita, Fred, 157
Yamashita, Masayuki, 158
Yamashita, Steve, 20
Yamazaki, Kazunori, 240
Yasuda, Joe R., 157
Yasui, Minoru, 10–11, 12, 79, 80, 82, 131–32, 147, 168–69
Yasui Community Award. *See* Minoru Yasui Community Award
Yeto, Mitsuru, 157
Yokoe, Merijane, 147
Yoko's restaurant, 167, 204, 239
Yokoyama-Reed, Ilene, 10
Yonemura, Hiroshi, 157
Yonezawa Women's College, 184
Yoritomo, Kent, 81, 82
Yoritomo, Sojiro, 125
Yoshida, Eiichi, 120
Yoshihara, Evelyn, 109–10
Yoshihara, Gene, 109–10
Yoshihara, Kumiko, 109
Yoshihara, Yasutaro, 109
Yoshihara-Sniff, Sandi, 110
Yoshimoto, Sang K. Yuh, 200–201
Young Insurance Agency, 107
Young People's Christian Conference, 61
Yunoki, Shiyoji, 157
YWCA, 109